THE EASY

3 INGREDIENT

COLLEGE
COOKBOOK

100 Quick, Low-Cost Recipes That Fit Your Budget AND Schedule!

Robin Fields

ADAMS MEDIA

NEW YORK   LONDON   TORONTO   SYDNEY   NEW DELHI

Adams Media
An Imprint of Simon & Schuster, LLC
100 Technology Center Drive
Stoughton, Massachusetts 02072

First Adams Media trade paperback
edition August 2024

ADAMS MEDIA and colophon are
registered trademarks of
Simon & Schuster, LLC.

Simon & Schuster: Celebrating 100 Years
of Publishing in 2024

For information about special discounts
for bulk purchases, please contact Simon
& Schuster Special Sales at 1-866-506-1949
or business@simonandschuster.com.

The Simon & Schuster Speakers Bureau
can bring authors to your live event. For
more information or to book an event,
contact the Simon & Schuster Speakers
Bureau at 1-866-248-3049 or visit our
website at www.simonspeakers.com.

Interior design and illustrations by
Kellie Emery
Photographs by James Stefiuk
Interior images © 123RF/lazartivan,
seregam

Manufactured in the United States
of America

10 9 8 7 6 5 4 3 2 1

Library of Congress Cataloging-in-
Publication Data
Names: Fields, Robin, author.
Title: The easy three-ingredient college
cookbook / Robin Fields.
Description: First Adams Media
trade paperback edition. | Stoughton,
Massachusetts: Adams Media, 2024. |
Includes index.
Identifiers: LCCN 2024007880 |
ISBN 9781507222492 (pb) | ISBN
9781507222508 (ebook)
Subjects: LCSH: Quick and easy cooking. |
Low budget cooking. | LCGFT: Cookbooks.
Classification: LCC TX833.5 .F53 2024 |
DDC 641.5/5--dc23/eng/20240304
LC record available at https://lccn.loc
.gov/2024007880

ISBN 978-1-5072-2249-2
ISBN 978-1-5072-2250-8 (ebook)

CONTENTS

INTRODUCTION

Cooking for yourself in college is a game changer! You don't need lots of expensive ingredients—just a handful of items can whip up a delicious (and cheap!) meal. When you're cramming for midterms, hosting a party in your dorm, trying to impress a date, or just avoiding the dining hall, your go-to recipes need to have easy-to-find ingredients and simple directions.

The Easy Three-Ingredient College Cookbook is full of fantastic meals you can make in no time flat! Whether you're cooking for the first time or you just want to make delicious and cheap meals, this book has you covered. Chapter 1 is a quick overview of cooking basics. You'll learn to read recipes, store ingredients, season food, and make sure your leftovers are still safe to eat. From there, you'll find one hundred quick, easy, and delicious recipes that will keep your roommates coming back for more!

Each recipe uses only three main ingredients, and not one of them requires a full kitchen setup. Say goodbye to running to the supermarket every time you want to cook. There's a good chance you already have all the necessary ingredients on hand! These recipes take staples and transform them into savory and craveable meals!

Have rolled oats, almond milk, and Greek yogurt in your dorm refrigerator? Try whipping up a hearty meal of Overnight Oats. Craving something a little more refined than campus food? Try the Vegetable Stir-Fry, made with frozen vegetables, bottled stir-fry sauce, and rice.

Craving a fun and easy dessert? Add vanilla ice cream, Oreos, and chocolate cookie pie crust to your shopping list for some delicious Oreo Ice Cream Pie.

Inside, you'll find a wide range of healthy and satisfying entrées, snacks, and desserts that will save you time. Many are microwave-friendly and portable, so you can eat on the go. With a quick prep and few ingredients, you can cook a nutritious meal in the time it takes for delivery to arrive (and for a fraction of the cost).

Save money by not eating out, and rely on this book's easy three-ingredient promise. So get ready to learn how to make trouble-free, affordable meals that you and your friends will love. It's time to get cooking!

CHAPTER 1

QUICK AND EASY COOKING IN A SMALL SPACE

Your living and cooking spaces may be limited, but that doesn't mean your meal options have to be. With few tools and a tight budget at your disposal, you may need to get a bit creative in the kitchen. However, after getting acquainted with the fundamentals of cooking for yourself and exploring the functions of your appliances, you'll likely find that creating uncomplicated yet satisfying home-cooked meals is well within your reach.

This chapter introduces you to a range of simple cooking options, offering helpful hints to take with you as you learn, and detailing some of the must-have accessories that will greatly improve your experience. Whether you're cooking for one or for a group of friends, this book has you covered. This chapter will serve as your go-to guide for basic food safety tips to help make sure you're preparing your meals and storing your leftovers properly. Additionally, this chapter gives you a basic overview of the ins and outs of cooking. Practice makes perfect, and as you learn more, you'll grow in confidence and ability to improvise. This chapter also talks about how the recipes deliver on the book's three-ingredient promise—excluding the essential salt, pepper, water, and, in Chapter 4, bread or a wrap. Finally, this book will focus on using a hot plate (or stove), a convection oven (or oven), a blender, and a microwave, as well as treats you can whip up without any appliances at all.

Why Cook for Yourself?

When you're in college, it may be especially tempting to order out, get your meals from nearby campus restaurants, or even buy a dining hall plan. However, from money saved to health consciousness, making your own food offers many advantages. Here are just a few of the reasons you'll want to make cooking for yourself a regular habit:

- **Easier than you think:** Your microwave, oven, blender, and hot plate are great tools to quickly transform your pantry ingredients into satisfying meals that you're actually excited to eat. Even if you're super busy or new to the kitchen, this book will offer you a plethora of new favorites that can be whipped up with very little prep and no prior culinary experience necessary.
- **Time saving:** Cooking for yourself means you don't have to wait to eat, or brave the elements to find something on campus. Having a fully stocked pantry and the tools you need to make something tasty ends up being the efficient option in the long run.
- **Cost effective:** Skipping takeout in favor of cooking at home drastically reduces your food budget. From the ability to buy your favorite things in bulk to saving on delivery fees, cooking for yourself is a great way to help foster your financial savvy.
- **Long-term benefits:** College is an excellent time to learn how to take care of yourself. Learning to navigate the kitchen will have positive impacts on your health and be a lifelong skill that improves over time.

Kitchen Essentials

Having this handful of cooking accessories in easy reach will greatly impact your enjoyment of making food at home. These items are useful for anyone starting their kitchen collection:

- **Pots and pans.** Having quality pots and pans is a must. It's tempting to buy budget sets, but many times those come with too many items and aren't what you need. A poor-quality pan causes uneven heating and can make food stick, causing havoc in cooking cleanup. Rather than purchase a set, choose a quality skillet or sauté pan with a lid and a medium-sized saucepan to get started. The majority of your recipes rely on these items, and they won't take up a lot of space. If you're using a hot plate, be sure that your pans fit it well. Oversized pans may cause accidental spills and uneven heating.
- **Bakeware.** Depending on how much you plan to cook, you may not need much bakeware. Again, avoid sets and opt for single, quality pieces that you can add to over time. To start, small (1-quart and 2-quart) casserole dishes are perfect for small portions. A standard muffin pan is also an excellent tool, and a rimmed baking sheet is perfect for everything from chicken to cookies. If you plan to bake frequently, you may find an 8" round baking pan is nonnegotiable.
- **Small tools.** While some dorms have a large kitchen to stock, others may lack space to work with. To start, look for a plastic spatula, a rubber spatula, tongs, a digital meat thermometer, and a whisk. If you enjoy a lot of soup, a large spoon or ladle can be a great investment as well. Consider the type of foods you frequently eat and what type of utensils are needed for those. And remember, you can always add to your collection over time as needed.

- **Spice rack.** Building your first spice rack or cabinet takes time. Rather than purchase a bunch of spices you might not use, start with a few simple ones and pick up more as you need them. Salt, pepper, oil, and nonstick cooking spray are a great starting point. Ground cinnamon, crushed red pepper flakes, and packets of pre-made taco and ranch seasoning also help add some flavor without taking up space. Over time, you will develop a preference for specific cooking oils and seasoning blends and can stock up.

Food Safety 101

For some, the kitchen and cooking may be second nature. But for others, college may be the first time you experience learning to cook. Beyond making your food taste amazing, learning a few basic food safety rules is very important. Besides fostering general cleanliness, these rules ensure that the food you eat is safe. Once you learn the basics, it's easy to integrate them into your kitchen routine to protect anyone you cook for.

- **Clean before and after cooking.** One thing that's easily forgotten, especially in a busy academic setting, is washing your hands. When you're on campus, you grab food on the go and don't think twice. However, it's good to practice handwashing before you handle any type of food. This prevents any germs from coming into contact with your food. When cooking, always ensure your hands, your tools, and your work area are clean. Pay special attention to the cleaning products you use, as some require sitting time to fully kill germs and often require a rinse with water before they're food safe. Cleaning up after you cook is just as important as when you begin. Clean your dishes, pans, and the areas where you cooked and ate. This reduces mess but also prevents food buildup that can attract pests.
- **Keep raw and cooked foods separate to avoid cross-contamination.** This food safety tip begins at the store. Be sure that you keep your raw meat away from fruits or vegetables as it may leak

onto them and contaminate them. In the refrigerator at home, place everything into grouped areas, and avoid stacking raw meat or eggs on top of things you don't intend to cook such as bread and fruit. If possible, keep meat in the bottom drawer so that if a leak occurs, it doesn't put your other food at risk. When you're cooking, raw meat should have a separate cutting board. Be sure that you wash your hands frequently when cutting meat and use a clean knife when cutting meat and transitioning to vegetables during the same session.

- **Always use a meat thermometer to determine doneness.** While there are visual cues you can rely on to ensure your meat is fully cooked, they're not always reliable. Regardless of your experience level, a meat thermometer will tell you exactly how warm the center of your food is and if it's safe to eat. Always measure the thickest part of your meat for accurate temperature. The cook times in this book are guidelines, but each oven and stovetop temperature may differ. If you're ever unsure if your food is done, add a few minutes to cooking time as needed and use visual cues.

- **Keep a close eye on your food while cooking.** Cooking times are excellent as a reference point, but it can be difficult to tell you precisely how long a food will take to cook. Not all ovens heat exactly the same, and you might be surprised to know that even the type of pan you use can slightly affect cook time. Cooking is an active activity, and while none of these recipes require a super sharp eye, it's important to set a time and check in on your food regularly. Aside from overcooking, unexpected boiling over or spilling can occur.

- **Put away your food promptly and always check the expiration dates.** Just as undercooked food can cause illness, so can food that's been left out for too long. Generally, two hours is the maximum amount of time that food should sit out. After this, it becomes more susceptible to bacteria growth. It's important to put away your leftover food promptly after finishing, cover it with plastic wrap or place it into an airtight container, and finish any leftovers within a few days to avoid mold and spoilage. It's also good practice to check the date on your food when you purchase it. While fruit and vegetables are usually fine in the refrigerator for days at a time, meat may require closer attention if the expiration date is near. You may even need to freeze it if you don't plan on eating it within a few days. Seafood, for example, spoils quickly and should be consumed within a day or two after purchase. In addition to checking the date, always look for signs of spoilage on your food such as discoloration, mold, or a bad smell.

Quick and Easy Cooking

Each recipe in this book is made up of simple, easy-to-find ingredients. It considers your busy schedule, so you won't be making anything overly complex, doing a lot of chopping, or making anything requiring special skills or equipment. This book combines pre-made food with a few tweaks to make it taste fresh and homemade. These recipes are meant to inspire you and give you confidence in the kitchen while not taking up a lot of time. As you begin sampling this collection of delicious dishes, following a few general guidelines will enhance your college cooking experience, especially if you're just learning your way around the kitchen. Here are some ways to make your meals easier than ever:

- **Start small:** Find a few simple recipes that you love and keep making them. Many of these recipes do not include toppings or garnishes but give you suggestions on how to make the dish your own. These suggestions will help you get comfortable with cooking for yourself and start cooking with confidence. Once you've got those recipes down, feel free to try spicing them up with creative additions, and start trying new recipes.

- **Read the entire recipe:** Read the whole recipe before you begin cooking. Collect and prepare all ingredients before beginning for a smooth cooking process. Many of these recipes cook very quickly and don't leave much time for finding ingredients once the process has started. Double-check that you have all ingredients in the correct size or amounts and have followed any ingredient notes, such as chopping an herb or melting butter, before you begin.
- **Simplify your ingredients:** This book uses a lot of pantry-stable and frozen ingredients to save you time. This eliminates the need for chopping and the worry of ingredients going bad before you can use them. During such a busy phase of life, it can be helpful to use pre-chopped vegetables and fruit as your budget allows. This will encourage you to get in the kitchen more and make healthy choices.
- **Clean as you cook:** Learning to cook for the first time can feel overwhelming. If you can learn to clean as you go, it will avoid the post-cooking mess that takes forever to clean up. To do this, you can make sure all trash is thrown away as you're done with it and wipe surfaces as you go. Whenever possible, cleaning the prep tools you used—such as knives and cutting boards—while the food is cooking can also save a lot of time. Keeping it under control little by little can prevent a larger mess that feels intimidating to clean up.
- **Keep learning:** Since cooking is a learning process, there may be times when you overcook something. It can be as simple as mushy pasta or a dark brown cookie, but it happens sometimes. In most cases, if you're watching your food closely during the cooking process, you're able to salvage the food and still enjoy it even if it's a little bit off. There may be times when, for any reason, a recipe just isn't a success for you. It's important to reread the recipe to troubleshoot where things went wrong and get back in the kitchen as quickly as possible to not lose confidence. Your next recipe could be a huge success; don't let one misstep stop you from enjoying the journey.

Pantry Staples

Each recipe in this book has three or fewer main ingredients, but also included are some extremely basic kitchen staples in addition to those three to help make sure the tastes and textures of your meals come out perfect. This book identifies a handful of staples that you likely already have in your kitchen. You will always want to have these on hand when creating the recipes in this book. These staples are:

- Salt
- Ground black pepper
- Water
- Bread (slices, pitas, tortillas, etc.) in Chapter 4

These must-haves were chosen for their versatility and frequent use not just in the recipes that follow, but also in the recipes you'll most commonly encounter online and in other cookbooks. If you're in the beginning stages of cultivating a spice rack, be sure to at least have salt and pepper on hand. You don't have to get too fancy too fast, but these seasonings will make a huge difference in the final flavors of many dishes.

With this information in hand, you are now ready to start cooking small batches in small spaces. Throughout the following chapters, you'll find plenty of simple and straightforward, delicious, three-ingredient recipes to suit all tastes. Don't be afraid to make mistakes, to try again if something doesn't quite work out, and to make space for creativity when the urge sets in. Use these recipes as your guide, and always feel free to customize dishes to your liking—just be aware that doing so will change the provided nutritional information.

CHAPTER 2

BREAKFAST

I t's a bit of a tired saying, but it's true: Breakfast is the most important meal of the day. However, once the busyness of college life sets in, it becomes increasingly tempting to skip your morning meal. Whether it's finals week, and you're running on no sleep, or you're balancing a heavy course load with an on-campus job, taking the time to nourish your body before heading out the door helps you a great deal. A solid breakfast keeps you full, focused, and performing at your very best.

Starting your day with quick and easy recipes that have you in and out of the kitchen in minutes will get your body fueled. It's much healthier than the shot of espresso you can grab from the campus café on the way to class. Plus, these recipes are easy enough that *anybody* can make them, regardless of skill level, and tasty enough that you're motivated to get out of bed to cook them. From the casual learner who wants a light bite on their way out the door, to the dedicated scholar that needs a full meal before their full schedule, you can find a recipe that suits your needs!

With classics like Fluffy Scrambled Eggs or Elevated Blueberry Muffins, and new weekend favorites like Shortcut French Toast and Everything Avocado Toast, this chapter is filled with recipes that will set you up on a sustainable and delicious breakfast routine.

Mango Sunrise Smoothie

Prep Time: 5 minutes **Cook Time:** N/A **Serves 1**

Start your day with this sweet and citrusy tropical smoothie. With Greek yogurt for protein and coconut milk for a creamy and delicious base, this easy, vitamin-rich breakfast comes together in no time. Add half a medium banana or a small drizzle of honey for an extra touch of natural sweetness. You can easily make this recipe your own by choosing a tropical blend of frozen fruit, switching up the Greek yogurt flavor for a complementary flavor (like pineapple), or using almond milk or oat milk if you prefer.

Ingredients

1 cup frozen mango chunks

1/2 cup low-fat vanilla Greek yogurt

1/2 cup coconut milk

Place all ingredients into a blender. Blend on high for 1 minute or until smooth and creamy. Serve immediately.

Per Serving: Calories: 387; Fat: 25g; Sodium: 51mg; Carbohydrates: 29g; Fiber: 2g; Sugar: 24g; Protein: 14g

Green Smoothie

Prep Time: 5 minutes **Cook Time:** N/A **Serves 1**

Loaded with spinach, kale, and a blend of ripe and refreshing fruit flavors, this simple smoothie is the perfect go-to for your busy mornings. By stocking your freezer with frozen fruit blends, you can reduce the ingredients needed to make a great smoothie without sacrificing flavor. Prepping is a breeze because the frozen fruit is pre-chopped. To round out the smoothie, coconut water offers a sweet, subtle nutty flavor. If coconut water isn't your thing, feel free to try unsweetened almond milk, orange juice, or water.

Ingredients

1 cup fresh baby spinach, loosely packed

1 cup coconut water

3/4 cup frozen Dole Fruit and Veggie Blends Berries n' Kale

1 Remove spinach stems by snapping them off or cutting them, and then place the spinach leaves into the blender. Add coconut water to the blender, and blend on high for 30 seconds or until no large pieces of spinach remain.

2 Add frozen fruit and vegetable mix to the blender and blend on high for 60 seconds. When done, fruit and vegetable pieces should be completely broken down. Serve immediately.

Per Serving: Calories: 116; Fat: 1g; Sodium: 277mg; Carbohydrates: 25g; Fiber: 6g; Sugar: 14g; Protein: 4g

Cheddar Egg Bites

Prep Time: 10 minutes **Cook Time:** 20 minutes **Makes 6** (serving size: 3 egg bites)

These simple homemade egg bites are better for your budget than the café alternative, have simple ingredients, and will keep your morning routine on track. Each bite is full of creamy, fluffy eggs and savory Cheddar. In addition, the cottage cheese and Cheddar combined with eggs makes this a protein-rich breakfast, which means you can look forward to staying satisfied and feeling full for longer. Feel free to add a tablespoon of chopped vegetables or cooked crumbled sausage to each egg cup to switch up the flavors a bit. Enjoy these egg bites with a dash of hot sauce for some added spiciness.

Ingredients

4 large eggs

⅓ cup small curd cottage cheese

¼ cup shredded sharp Cheddar cheese

½ teaspoon salt

1 Preheat the oven to 350°F. Spray six cups of a muffin tin with nonstick cooking spray.

2 Place all ingredients into a blender. Blend on high for 20 seconds or until smooth. Pour egg mixture evenly into each prepared cup in the muffin tin—they will be about three-quarters full.

3 Place the muffin tin into the oven and bake for 20 minutes. When done, egg bites will appear firm in the center and edges will be slightly browned. Serve warm. Store leftover egg bites in an airtight container in the refrigerator for up to 3 days.

Per Serving: Calories: 236; Fat: 14g; Sodium: 950mg; Carbohydrates: 2g; Fiber: 0g; Sugar: 1g; Protein: 20g

Everything Avocado Toast

Prep Time: 5 minutes **Cook Time:** 2 minutes **Serves 1**

Avocado toast is a great morning meal; it's full of healthy fats, which help keep you feeling full. Everything but the Bagel seasoning is made up of a delicious blend of sesame seeds, onion, garlic, and salt—just what an avocado needs to perk up its natural creamy goodness. Sourdough bread is ideal for this recipe because it has a big crunch and natural sour flavor, and it won't get soggy from the avocado. Keep the other half of your avocado fresh by lightly spraying nonstick cooking spray on it and wrapping it tightly in plastic. Store in the refrigerator until ready to eat, within 2 days.

Ingredients

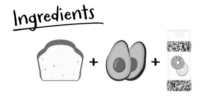

1 slice The Rustik Oven Sourdough Bread

½ medium avocado, peeled and pitted

2 teaspoons Everything but the Bagel Sesame Seasoning Blend

1 Toast bread in a toaster until golden brown and set aside.

2 Place avocado into a small bowl and mash with a fork until only a few chunks remain. Spread over toast in an even layer.

3 Sprinkle avocado toast with Everything but the Bagel seasoning and serve.

Per Serving: Calories: 333; Fat: 11g; Sodium: 955mg; Carbohydrates: 38g; Fiber: 7g; Sugar: 1g; Protein: 8g

Fluffy Scrambled Eggs

Prep Time: 5 minutes **Cook Time:** 5 minutes **Serves 1**

The key to good scrambled eggs is to remove them from your hot plate or stove before they overcook. Cooking over a low, even heat allows the eggs to scramble without drying out or tasting rubbery. Adding dairy, such as sour cream—or, alternatively, milk—helps eggs retain moisture and makes them more forgiving so you can count on delicious, fluffy eggs every time. Once you've mastered the base, you can get creative by adding sautéed vegetables such as bell peppers and onions and even a teaspoon of freshly chopped herbs, such as chives, to brighten up the dish.

Ingredients

2 large eggs

2 tablespoons sour cream

¼ teaspoon salt

1 tablespoon salted butter

1 In a medium bowl, whisk eggs for 2 minutes or until well combined and small air bubbles form over top of eggs. Whisk in sour cream and salt until fully combined.

2 In a skillet over medium-low heat, melt butter. Once halfway melted, pour in eggs. Use a rubber spatula to gently stir eggs in a figure-eight pattern. Run the spatula along the sides of the skillet and push eggs to the center before doing another figure-eight pattern. Once eggs begin to firm up (about 2 minutes), turn off the heat.

3 With the heat off, continue stirring eggs in the same pattern, then scrape the sides until eggs are firm and mostly set. Use the spatula to break eggs into small bite-sized pieces as needed. Serve warm.

Per Serving: Calories: 290; Fat: 24g; Sodium: 825mg; Carbohydrates: 1g; Fiber: 0g; Sugar: 1g; Protein: 13g

Salsa Breakfast Skillet

Prep Time: 5 minutes **Cook Time:** 15 minutes **Serves 1**

If you love the combination of flavors found in traditional breakfast burritos, this easy skillet meal belongs in your weekly rotation. Fluffy eggs and savory sausage make up the bulk of this recipe, but the zesty salsa instantly adds a pop of color and depth of flavor without the need for chopping any vegetables. Enjoy this dish as a bowl meal with a sprinkle of cheese and sour cream, or wrap it up in a tortilla for a quick, on-the-go breakfast. Feel free to use cooked and crumbled bacon or cubed ham in place of the sausage.

Ingredients

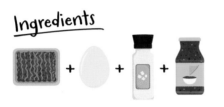

2 ounces ground pork breakfast sausage

2 large eggs

¼ teaspoon salt

¼ cup mild chunky salsa

1 In a nonstick skillet over medium heat, use a spatula to crumble sausage into small pieces, and brown sausage until no pink remains, about 7 minutes.

2 Drain any grease from sausage into a container that can withstand the heat, and return the skillet to the stovetop over medium heat.

3 In a small bowl, whisk eggs with salt and then pour into the skillet with sausage. Use the spatula to push eggs around the skillet until they begin to resemble scrambled eggs, being sure to break apart large pieces. Stir in salsa until just combined and serve.

Per Serving: Calories: 281; Fat: 16g; Sodium: 1,220mg; Carbohydrates: 5g; Fiber: 2g; Sugar: 4g; Protein: 24g

Big Batch Sausage and Cheese Biscuit Sandwiches

Prep Time: 5 minutes **Cook Time:** 37 minutes **Makes 8** (serving size: 1 sandwich)

When the craving for something hearty and delicious hits, there's no need for a trip to the drive-through. Delicious frozen biscuits bake up in just over 20 minutes for the perfect breakfast sandwich. This big batch will keep your freezer stocked with a quick meal for whenever the mood strikes. And you don't have to stick to the basic creation; this is a great recipe to flex your creativity. Feel free to add a fried egg to the sandwiches or use strips of cooked bacon. Alternatively, bagels and English muffins also work great in this recipe and don't need to be pre-baked.

Ingredients

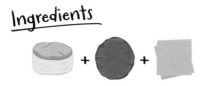

8 frozen Pillsbury Grands! Southern Homestyle Buttermilk Biscuits

8 frozen Johnsonville Sandwich Size Breakfast Sausage Patties

8 (1-ounce) slices mild Cheddar cheese

1 Preheat the oven to 375°F. Line a baking sheet with parchment paper.

2 Place biscuits in rows on the baking sheet so that the edges touch. Bake for 25 minutes or until biscuits are golden brown on top. Set aside to cool for 10 minutes.

3 Reduce oven temperature to 350°F. Line a second baking sheet with parchment paper.

4 Arrange sausage patties in a single layer on the prepared baking sheet. Bake for 12 minutes, turning once during cooking time.

5 To assemble sandwiches, cut open biscuits and place a sausage patty on the bottom half of each biscuit. Add a slice of cheese and the top half of each biscuit.

continued on next page

6 To store: Allow sandwiches to cool completely. Then, wrap each sandwich in aluminum foil. Refrigerate for up to 4 days. To freeze: Place the foil-wrapped sandwiches into a freezer-safe zip-top bag and freeze for up to 3 months.

7 To reheat from the refrigerator: Remove sandwich from foil and wrap in a damp paper towel. Microwave for 1 minute or until heated through. For frozen sandwiches: Follow the same process, but microwave for 2 minutes and 30 seconds.

Per Serving: Calories: 485; Fat: 31g; Sodium: 1,292mg; Carbohydrates: 26g; Fiber: 0g; Sugar: 2g; Protein: 20g

Banana Nut Oatmeal

Prep Time: 5 minutes **Cook Time:** 1 minute 30 seconds **Serves 1**

This recipe elevates the classic packet oatmeal breakfast to the next level. Adding a few simple ingredients can take an ordinary oatmeal from "just okay" to "outstanding," creating a delicious and filling meal with minimal extra effort. Fresh banana is mixed into this comforting dish for flavor, and chopped nuts add a satisfying crunch to every bite. This recipe uses only half of a banana, but don't let the rest go to waste. Completely peel it, then slice it and place into a small freezer-safe zip-top bag and freeze it, so you can easily add it to your next smoothie. Or, use the leftover fresh banana slices to decorate the top of your oatmeal.

Ingredients

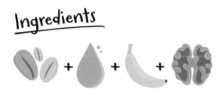

1 (1.51-ounce) packet instant cinnamon spice oatmeal

2/3 cup water

1/2 medium banana, mashed

1 tablespoon chopped walnuts

1 Empty oatmeal packet into a medium microwave-safe bowl. Pour in water and stir to combine.

2 Microwave for 1 minute 30 seconds, then stir. Oatmeal should be tender and creamy. Mix in mashed banana until combined. Sprinkle the top of oatmeal with walnuts, then serve warm.

Per Serving: Calories: 256; Fat: 6g; Sodium: 178mg; Carbohydrates: 46g; Fiber: 6g; Sugar: 16g; Protein: 6g

Baking Sheet Peanut Butter Granola

Prep Time: 5 minutes **Cook Time:** 20 minutes **Makes 2 cups** (serving size: $^{1}/_{4}$ cup)

Whether it's layered between yogurt and fruit in a parfait or enjoyed as a quick sweet snack, granola offers a satisfying combination of flavor and texture. Making personalized granola allows you to control the ingredients in it, so whether you're avoiding excessive sugar or want to tailor it exactly to your liking, this recipe is ideal. Make this granola all your own by swapping out the peanut butter for your favorite nut butter such as cashew or almond. Once it's cooled, you can mix in dried fruit, mini chocolate chips, coconut flakes, or toasted chopped nuts for even more flavor.

Ingredients

$^{1}/_{4}$ cup creamy peanut butter

2 cups rolled oats

1 teaspoon ground cinnamon

1 Preheat the oven to 325°F.

2 Place peanut butter into a large microwave-safe bowl and warm it in the microwave for 30 seconds. Stir, then add oats and cinnamon, and mix until all oats are well coated.

3 Line a baking sheet with parchment paper and scrape oat mixture onto the parchment. Bake granola for 20 minutes, stirring halfway through cooking time, until golden brown.

4 Remove granola from the oven and allow it to cool for at least 30 minutes. It will become crunchy as it cools. Break apart any large chunks into bite-sized pieces and store in an airtight container for up to 2 weeks.

Per Serving: Calories: 123; Fat: 5g; Sodium: 34mg; Carbohydrates: 16g; Fiber: 3g; Sugar: 1g; Protein: 4g

Overnight Oats

Prep Time: 5 minutes **Cook Time:** N/A **Serves 2**

This is one of the easiest breakfast meal prep recipes! It can be made up to three days in advance, and customized with your favorite toppings to keep your breakfast exciting. Oats are already a filling option; adding Greek yogurt's protein will help keep you powered up throughout the morning. This recipe uses almond milk for its nutty undertones, but feel free to swap it out with any type of milk that you have on hand. These oats are a great base and can be dressed up with diced berries, or chopped nuts can add a delightful crunch.

Ingredients

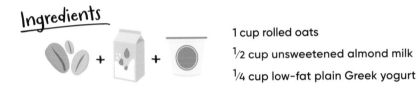

1 cup rolled oats

½ cup unsweetened almond milk

¼ cup low-fat plain Greek yogurt

In a microwave-safe container with a lid, mix all ingredients until well combined. Put the lid on the container and place it into the refrigerator for at least 4 hours, or up to 3 days. Oats will be softened and creamy when ready to eat. Enjoy them cold or place the container into the microwave for 15 seconds at a time, stirring between intervals until warmed.

Per Serving: Calories: 178; Fat: 4g; Sodium: 54mg; Carbohydrates: 29g; Fiber: 4g; Sugar: 2g; Protein: 8g

Strawberry Chia Seed Pudding

Prep Time: 5 minutes **Cook Time:** N/A **Serves 1**

This nutritious breakfast pudding is topped with fruit preserves for a sweet and tangy combination that pairs wonderfully with the subtle vanilla undertones. While very small when dry, chia seeds expand drastically in liquid. Plan at least 30 minutes ahead when making this recipe to ensure enough time for them to expand. Alternatively, you can mix up this pudding and leave it in the refrigerator overnight. With just 2 tablespoons of chia seeds, this recipe packs nearly 10 grams of fiber, a good portion of the recommended daily amount.

Ingredients

2 tablespoons chia seeds

½ cup unsweetened vanilla almond milk

2 tablespoons strawberry preserves

1 Using an 8-ounce Mason jar, mix chia seeds and almond milk until well combined.

2 Put the lid on the jar and place into the refrigerator for 30 minutes, then stir again to break up any clumps.

3 Top with strawberry preserves and replace the lid. Let chill for at least 2 more hours or overnight (up to 2 days). Serve chilled.

Per Serving: Calories: 271; Fat: 10g; Sodium: 106mg; Carbohydrates: 41g; Fiber: 11g; Sugar: 20g; Protein: 6g

Shortcut French Toast

Prep Time: 10 minutes **Cook Time:** 6 minutes **Serves 1**

Melting ice cream is the ultimate French toast hack. Ice cream is typically made of cream or milk, sugar, vanilla, and egg yolks, similar to the main ingredients in any French toast. Rather than gathering together all of these ingredients, you can simply melt down some ice cream for dipping your bread and get beautiful golden brown French toast. Feel free to try unique ice creams such as butter pecan or coffee for some added flavor. Then, top your creative breakfast masterpiece with maple syrup and powdered sugar or sliced strawberries and whipped cream.

Ingredients

½ cup vanilla ice cream

¼ teaspoon ground cinnamon

2 (1"-thick) slices Texas toast

1 Place ice cream into a medium microwave-safe bowl and microwave for 30 seconds or until melted. Mix with cinnamon until well combined.

2 Press each slice of bread into ice cream mixture on both sides. Let sit to soak for 5 minutes.

3 Warm a skillet over medium heat, then spray with nonstick cooking spray. Carefully place soaked bread slices into the warm skillet and fry on each side for 3 minutes. When done, French toast should be golden brown on each side. Serve warm.

Per Serving: Calories: 255; Fat: 5g; Sodium: 369mg; Carbohydrates: 43g; Fiber: 2g; Sugar: 11g; Protein: 7g

Elevated Blueberry Muffins

Prep Time: 5 minutes **Cook Time:** 12 minutes **Makes 6** (serving size: 1 muffin)

Muffin mixes are extremely budget-friendly, great for keeping in the pantry, and only require a few extra ingredients to transform them. This recipe adds fresh blueberries for a mix of fresh fruit flavor alongside the more artificial flavors from traditional muffin mix. Rather than milk, this recipe uses yogurt to add a bit of tang and brighten the batch. If you enjoy lemon, try lemon-flavored Greek yogurt for a bright burst of flavor, or mix in a tablespoon of lemon zest. You can switch up the muffin mix for another flavor such as cinnamon sugar to keep things interesting.

Ingredients

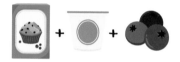

1 (7-ounce) package Martha White Blueberry Muffin Mix

½ cup low-fat plain Greek yogurt

½ cup fresh blueberries

1 Preheat the oven to 425°F. Line six cups of a muffin tin with paper liners and set aside.

2 In a large bowl, stir muffin mix and yogurt until well combined. Gently stir in blueberries.

3 Pour mixture evenly into each lined cup in the muffin tin—they will each be about two-thirds full.

4 Place the muffin tin into the oven and bake for 12 minutes or until muffins are browned at the edges and a toothpick inserted into the center comes out with just a few crumbs.

5 Allow muffins to cool for 10 minutes before serving. Store leftover muffins in an airtight container in the refrigerator for up to 3 days.

Per Serving: Calories: 151; Fat: 3g; Sodium: 166mg; Carbohydrates: 28g; Fiber: 0g; Sugar: 15g; Protein: 3g

Crescent Roll Sausages

Prep Time: 5 minutes **Cook Time:** 12 minutes **Makes 8** (serving size: 2 rolls)

Crescent rolls make a great breakfast shortcut and add a filling bready element to your morning meal! Savory breakfast sausage and buttery crescent rolls make an excellent pairing for a flaky and succulent bite. If you like mixing sweet and savory for breakfast, feel free to swap with maple-flavored sausage or dip the finished rolls in maple syrup. These sausage rolls can be prepared at the beginning of the week and reheated in the microwave for 1 minute to enjoy. Store leftover sandwiches in an airtight container in the refrigerator for up to 3 days.

Ingredients

1 (8-ounce) can 8-count crescent rolls

8 fresh Johnsonville Original Recipe Breakfast Sausage Links

1 Preheat the oven to 375°F. Line a baking sheet with parchment paper.

2 On a clean work surface, open can of crescent rolls and unroll each triangle.

3 On the widest edge of roll, place one sausage. Roll up each crescent roll, starting at the end with sausage and rolling toward the smallest point. Some sausage will still be visible.

4 Place sausage rolls on the prepared baking sheet. Bake for 12 minutes or until the rolls are golden brown and the sausage has an internal temperature of at least 145°F. Let cool for 5 minutes, then serve.

Per Serving: Calories: 308; Fat: 19g; Sodium: 731mg; Carbohydrates: 26g; Fiber: 0g; Sugar: 7g; Protein: 10g

CHAPTER 3

SNACKS AND SMALL PLATES

Everyone is familiar with the sensation of being hungry, but not quite hungry enough for an entire meal—this chapter is dedicated to those moments. Whether it's in between lunch and dinner, after a sports practice or club meeting, or late at night when you're catching up on your shows, having the right snacks on hand is one of the best remedies for that "hangry" feeling that we all know too well.

The best snacks and small plates are satisfying and very convenient. So, it's tempting to rely on pre-packaged and generally unhealthy convenience foods to tackle any cravings that arise as quickly as possible. The good news is, there's a better way to keep yourself from mindlessly grazing, and this brighter path will satisfy your taste buds, save you money, and keep your body feeling good.

This chapter will show you how to make a variety of easy, small-portioned bites to keep those temptations at bay. From savory Salsa Cream Cheese Pinwheels to White Queso that tastes as good as from a restaurant, get ready to meet your new favorite recipes for whenever your appetite needs satisfying.

Buffalo Chicken Dip

Prep Time: 5 minutes **Cook Time:** 1 minute **Serves 1**

Canned chicken is a versatile, inexpensive, and shelf-stable ingredient that is often ignored. Stocking up on canned foods like this chicken gives you the flexibility to eat a meal at home without the concern of fresh meat sitting in the refrigerator for too long. You can whip up this creamy and spicy dip to enjoy warm or cold alongside tortilla chips or celery sticks for a delicious and flavorful snack at a moment's notice.

Ingredients

1 (5-ounce) can chunk chicken breast in water, drained

2 ounces cream cheese, softened

3 tablespoons Frank's RedHot Buffalo Wings Sauce

1 Place chicken on a cutting board and chop into bite-sized pieces. Transfer to a medium bowl.

2 Add cream cheese and buffalo wing sauce to the bowl and mix well until evenly thick and pink.

3 For cold dip: Enjoy right away or refrigerate for 20 minutes. For warm dip: Microwave for 1 minute, stir well, and serve warm.

Per Serving: Calories: 302; Fat: 19g; Sodium: 2,244mg; Carbohydrates: 2g; Fiber: 0g; Sugar: 2g; Protein: 26g

Hummus

Prep Time: 5 minutes **Cook Time:** N/A **Makes 2 cups** (serving size: 2 tablespoons)

Fresh hummus is incredibly simple to make and doesn't even require cooking! It's a protein-rich snack that goes well with crackers and fresh vegetables.

Ingredients

1 (15-ounce) can chickpeas, drained and rinsed

2 tablespoons no-sugar-added creamy peanut butter

2 tablespoons fresh lemon juice

¼ teaspoon salt

Place all ingredients into a blender. Blend on high for 45 seconds or until smooth and creamy, then serve. Refrigerate leftovers in an airtight container for up to 3 days.

Per Serving: Calories: 34; Fat: 1g; Sodium: 69mg; Carbohydrates: 4g; Fiber: 1g; Sugar: 1g; Protein: 2g

Chicken and Spinach Dip

Prep Time: 5 minutes **Cook Time:** 2 minutes **Makes 1 cup** (serving size: ½ cup)

Pre-made dips are loaded with flavor, and their convenience can't be beat. This recipe adds protein for a satisfying snack and takes only minutes to make!

Ingredients

½ cup La Terra Fina Spinach Artichoke & Parmesan Dip & Spread

½ cup cold chopped rotisserie chicken

¼ cup shredded mozzarella cheese

Mix all ingredients in a medium microwave-safe bowl. Microwave for 2 minutes and then stir. When done, cheese should be melted and chicken should be heated through. Serve warm.

Per Serving: Calories: 245; Fat: 17g; Sodium: 534mg; Carbohydrates: 5g; Fiber: 2g; Sugar: 2g; Protein: 17g

Salsa Cream Cheese Pinwheels

Prep Time: 5 minutes **Cook Time:** N/A **Serves 1**

When you're craving a late-night snack, these pinwheels are satisfying without feeling heavy. They come together in minutes for a delicious and creamy nosh. Feel free to add ¼ cup of shredded cooked chicken or a sprinkle of cheese to transform these into a full meal. You can also heat them in a skillet when fully assembled, for a few minutes on each side. This lightly melts the cream cheese and brings out a deeper flavor profile. If you're not a fan of salsa, feel free to omit it and add pepperoni or slices of deli turkey.

Ingredients

2 ounces cream cheese, softened

⅓ cup mild salsa

1 (8") flour tortilla

1 In a small bowl, mix cream cheese and salsa until well combined.

2 Place tortilla on a plate. Spread cream cheese mixture evenly across one side of tortilla, spreading to the edges.

3 Starting with the edge closest to you, tightly roll tortilla into a log and press firmly to seal. Place the seam-side down and cut tortilla into 1"-wide slices. Serve.

Per Serving: Calories: 357; Fat: 19g; Sodium: 1,166mg; Carbohydrates: 33g; Fiber: 4g; Sugar: 9g; Protein: 7g

Bacon-Wrapped Jalapeño Poppers

Prep Time: 10 minutes **Cook Time:** 15 minutes **Makes 8** (serving size: 4 poppers)

Rather than coating these jalapeño poppers in flour and breadcrumbs, which can be messy and time-consuming, this recipe simply wraps them in bacon. Not only does it add loads of smoky flavor, but it simplifies the process. Feel free to let your creativity shine and add ¼ cup of your favorite shredded cheese to these poppers, or add ¼ teaspoon of garlic powder or dry ranch seasoning for a zesty kick. If you have sensitive skin, consider wearing gloves while you handle the peppers, as their natural oils can cause irritation and redness for some people. Then, remove the gloves and wash your hands thoroughly before touching your face.

Ingredients

4 medium jalapeños

4 tablespoons cream cheese, softened

4 slices bacon, cut in half crosswise

1 Preheat the oven to 400°F. Line a baking sheet with parchment paper and set aside.

2 Slice each jalapeño in half lengthwise. Use a spoon to scrape out seeds and white membrane from each pepper.

3 Stuff each pepper half with ½ tablespoon cream cheese, pressing down slightly to pack it. Wrap each popper tightly with bacon and secure it with a toothpick.

4 Place poppers on the prepared baking sheet, leaving a couple of inches of space between each popper. Bake for 15 minutes or until bacon is fully cooked and peppers are softened. Let cool for 10 minutes and serve.

Per Serving: Calories: 195; Fat: 15g; Sodium: 461mg; Carbohydrates: 3g; Fiber: 1g; Sugar: 2g; Protein: 8g

White Queso

Prep Time: 5 minutes **Cook Time:** 8 minutes
Makes 2 cups (serving size: 2 tablespoons)

Bad news for your favorite local Mexican restaurant—re-creating this delicious snack in your own kitchen is easy! Perfect for game day, or any time a craving for tasty Tex-Mex arises, this cheesy dip is sure to be a crowd pleaser. Enjoy it with warmed tortilla chips or pour it on top of nachos piled with your favorite ingredients for a delicious and budget-friendly alternative to takeout. You may want to prepare a double batch just to make sure you don't run out! Look for canned evaporated milk in the grocery store aisle with baking items like flour.

Ingredients

¼ pound white American cheese, chopped

½ cup evaporated milk

2 tablespoons drained canned diced green chilies

1. Place all ingredients into a skillet over medium heat. Stir continuously until cheese is fully melted and queso is smooth, about 8 minutes. When done, queso should be able to coat the back of a spoon.

2. Place queso into a serving bowl and serve warm.

3. Store leftovers in the refrigerator in an airtight container for up to 3 days. To reheat, microwave for 30 seconds and stir; then continue heating for up to ten additional 1-second increments as needed.

Per Serving: Calories: 34; Fat: 2g; Sodium: 105mg; Carbohydrates: 2g; Fiber: 0g; Sugar: 0g; Protein: 2g

Peanut Butter and Banana Rice Cakes

Prep Time: 5 minutes **Cook Time:** N/A **Serves 1**

This snack satisfies your need for a salty, crunchy, and sweet treat all at once. Rice cakes are often viewed as a boring food, but adding exciting toppings turns them into an amazing snack. The soft bites of banana contrast nicely with the rice cake, and peanut butter adds lots of great flavor. You can customize these by using your favorite rice cake flavors such as caramel or chocolate. Also, you can add berries or a sprinkle of ground cinnamon to your rice cake, or use Nutella in place of peanut butter.

Ingredients

2 tablespoons no-sugar-added creamy peanut butter

1 Quaker Lightly Salted Rice Cake

1 medium banana, sliced into ¼"-thick slices

Spread peanut butter into an even layer on rice cake. Top with banana slices and serve.

Per Serving: Calories: 320; Fat: 15g; Sodium: 71mg; Carbohydrates: 41g; Fiber: 6g; Sugar: 16g; Protein: 9g

Garlic Cheesy Breadsticks

Prep Time: 5 minutes **Cook Time:** 15 minutes **Makes 12** (serving size: 2 breadsticks)

You won't have to chop any garlic to enjoy this cheesy herbaceous dish. A flavorful spread gives these breadsticks high-impact flavor with a fraction of the effort. Pre-made pizza dough makes it easier than ever to re-create this savory and delicious pizza restaurant favorite. Add a sprinkle of grated Parmesan and dip them into warmed pizza sauce for a true indulgence. And if you'd like to make your own garlic spread, simply mix ¼ cup of softened salted butter with 1 teaspoon of minced garlic.

Ingredients

1 (13.8-ounce) tube refrigerated Pillsbury Classic Pizza Crust

¼ cup Land O' Lakes Garlic & Herb Butter Spread, softened

2 cups shredded mozzarella cheese

1 Preheat the oven to 425°F. Line a baking sheet with parchment paper.

2 Unroll pizza dough onto the prepared baking sheet. Press dough with your fingers until it's about ¼" thick. Drop spoonfuls of garlic and herb spread over the dough. Smooth into a thin even layer.

3 Sprinkle mozzarella evenly over dough. Bake for 15 minutes or until cheese is melted and golden brown. Use a sharp knife to cut into twelve breadsticks by cutting dough in half and then cutting each half into six pieces. Serve warm.

Per Serving: Calories: 294; Fat: 12g; Sodium: 643mg; Carbohydrates: 35g; Fiber: 0g; Sugar: 5g; Protein: 12g

Guacamole

Prep Time: 5 minutes **Cook Time:** N/A **Serves 2**

Whether you're enjoying it alongside tortilla chips or with a zesty taco bowl, this easy guacamole goes well with all of your favorite Mexican-style dishes. When shopping for avocados, look for ones with a medium firmness, not overly squishy or hard. Popping off the stem on the outside of the avocado should reveal a golden green color when it's ripe. If the stem doesn't come off easily or is pale in color, the avocado isn't yet ripe. Dark brown colors indicate that it's overripe and beginning to spoil. Those avocados should be avoided, as they will quickly ruin your guacamole.

Ingredients

2 medium avocados, peeled, halved, and pitted

¼ cup fresh Del Monte Pico de Gallo, drained

Juice of 1 small lime

¼ teaspoon salt

1 Scoop avocado out of its skin and into a medium bowl. Use a fork to mash until only a few chunks remain.

2 Add pico de gallo, lime juice, and salt to the bowl. Gently stir to combine, then serve.

Per Serving: Calories: 238; Fat: 19g; Sodium: 681mg; Carbohydrates: 14g; Fiber: 9g; Sugar: 1g; Protein: 3g

Microwave Kettle Corn

Prep Time: 5 minutes **Cook Time:** 2 minutes **Serves 1**

Enjoy this classic carnival food right at home with just a few simple ingredients. Sweet and salty meet for this delicious, easy-to-make snack. A brown paper lunch bag acts as the popcorn bag for this recipe, but you can also make it in a glass or silicone microwave popcorn maker. This popcorn makes an excellent addition to a snack mix, too. Simply add a few tablespoons of your choice of pretzels, M&M's, or roasted almonds for a satisfying and tasty treat. You can use these directions to make classic buttered popcorn as well; simply omit the sugar and finish your batch with a tablespoon of melted butter and a generous sprinkle of salt.

Ingredients

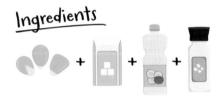

2 tablespoons yellow popcorn kernels

1 teaspoon granulated sugar

1 teaspoon vegetable oil

1/8 teaspoon salt

1 Shake all ingredients together in a brown paper lunch bag. Fold the bag over to secure it closed.

2 Place the bag into the microwave and cook for 2 minutes. Popcorn will begin popping after a minute and quickly increase in popping speed as the bag fills. When the popping slows, popcorn will be ready. If it slows before 2 minutes is up, remove bag from the microwave early to prevent burning. Allow to sit for 3 minutes before opening the bag. To serve, pour popcorn into a bowl, careful to avoid hot steam.

Per Serving: Calories: 180; Fat: 6g; Sodium: 292mg; Carbohydrates: 29g; Fiber: 5g; Sugar: 4g; Protein: 4g

CHAPTER 4

SANDWICHES AND WRAPS

This chapter will help you take control of your wallet and put an end to your excessive food-ordering habit once and for all! Sure, pressing a few buttons on your phone to commandeer a sandwich or wrap is easy. However, your food options are much more customizable when you learn how to make your favorites at home. You can have all of your favorite options on demand, without paying delivery fees. Plus, preparing your own meals gives you a lifelong skill, and knowing exactly which ingredients are going into your foods helps you make better decisions.

Because bread and tortillas are staple ingredients for sandwiches and wraps, recipes in this chapter do **not** include them as one of this book's three-count of main ingredients. As a result, you'll get a more well-rounded flavor into every bite. As always, feel free to swap ingredients for taste, and use what you have on hand as necessary. Every ingredient in these recipes might not be your preference, but you can use the recipes as a guide and build off of them. From a fresh and savory BLT Salad Wrap to a warm and gooey Tuna Melt, this chapter is filled to the brim with easy and satisfying ideas.

BLT Salad Wrap

Prep Time: 10 minutes **Cook Time:** N/A **Serves 1**

Salad kits don't have to be limited to bowls; they also make a convenient filling for sandwiches and wraps. Grabbing a few salad kits each week gives you the flexibility to make a quick meal without chopping or taking out a long list of ingredients. The salad kit used for this recipe comes with a delicious and creamy avocado dressing that ties all the ingredients together in this quick meal. Feel free to add extra vegetables or more protein such as rotisserie chicken for days when you're feeling extra hungry.

Ingredients

1 (6.5-ounce) package Taylor Farms BLT Salad Kit with Chicken & Bacon

1 (10") Mission Garden Spinach Herb Wrap

1 Open salad kit and place lettuce in the kit's bowl. Top with bacon, cheese, and chicken. Drizzle with dressing and toss to coat.

2 Place wrap on a flat surface. Pour salad onto the center of wrap. Begin rolling one side into a cylinder, tucking in the ends as you go.

3 With the seam down, cut wrap in half using a diagonal horizontal cut across the center. Serve.

Per Serving: Calories: 510; Fat: 28g; Sodium: 1,250mg; Carbohydrates: 48g; Fiber: 6g; Sugar: 6g; Protein: 20g

Hummus and Vegetable Sandwich

Prep Time: 5 minutes **Cook Time:** N/A **Serves 1**

Thick and creamy hummus makes an amazing, protein-packed sandwich. This super fresh tasting sandwich won't leave you feeling bogged down, but it will definitely keep you full throughout your day. And, as an added nutritional bonus, the whole-wheat bread in this recipe provides dietary fiber to make this meal even more satiating when paired with the vegetables. For a fun cooking challenge, skip the store-bought hummus and make your own from the simple recipe in Chapter 3!

Ingredients

2 tablespoons hummus

2 ($^3/_4$") slices whole-wheat bread

2 ($^1/_4$"-thick) slices beefsteak tomato

4 ($^1/_4$"-thick) cucumber slices

1 Spread hummus onto one side of each piece of bread.

2 Place tomato slices onto one slice of hummus-coated bread, then stack cucumbers on top. Top sandwich with other slice of bread. Cut sandwich in half and serve.

Per Serving: Calories: 228; Fat: 5g; Sodium: 407mg; Carbohydrates: 36g; Fiber: 7g; Sugar: 5g; Protein: 11g

Tuna Melt

Prep Time: 5 minutes **Cook Time:** 8 minutes **Serves 1**

Canned and pouch tuna are great pantry staples to regularly keep on hand. While you might think of tuna salad as being cold, warming it up for a satisfying melt is a wonderful spin that only takes one extra step. Golden crispy bread paired with the savory tuna and boldness of Cheddar makes the perfect bite for this handheld entrée that comes together in less than 15 minutes.

Ingredients

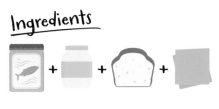

1 (2.6-ounce) pouch chunk light tuna

2 tablespoons mayonnaise, divided

2 (^{3}/4") slices white sandwich bread

1 (1-ounce) slice mild Cheddar cheese

1 Warm a nonstick skillet over medium heat.

2 In a small bowl, mix tuna and 1 tablespoon mayonnaise. Spread remaining mayonnaise onto one side of each slice of bread.

3 Place slices of bread on a clean work surface, mayonnaise-coated sides facing down. Spoon tuna mixture onto one slice of bread. Place cheese on top of tuna and top sandwich with the other slice of bread, with mayonnaise side facing up.

4 Place sandwich into the skillet and cook for 4 minutes on each side until bread is golden brown and cheese is melted. Cut in half and serve warm.

Per Serving: Calories: 530; Fat: 31g; Sodium: 949mg; Carbohydrates: 30g; Fiber: 2g; Sugar: 4g; Protein: 29g

Sourdough Grilled Cheese

Prep Time: 5 minutes **Cook Time:** 8 minutes **Serves 2** (serving size: ¹⁄2 sandwich)

Grilled cheese is a classic go-to, but with a few simple swaps, you can take it to the next level. Quality sourdough will give your sandwich a more refined taste than plain sandwich bread. Additionally, bold Cheddar and creamy American cheese combine for that picture-perfect cheese pull, but with more flavor than either can offer alone. Opt for fresh deli-sliced American cheese to avoid the plastic-like taste that some pre-sliced cheeses have.

Ingredients

2 tablespoons mayonnaise

2 slices The Rustik Oven Sourdough Bread

2 (1-ounce) slices American cheese

2 (1-ounce) slices sharp Cheddar cheese

1 Warm a nonstick skillet over medium heat. Spread mayonnaise onto one side of each piece of bread.

2 Place one slice of bread, mayonnaise-side down, into the skillet. Arrange cheese slices on bread. Top with remaining slice of bread, with mayonnaise side facing up.

3 Cook on each side for 4 minutes or until deep golden brown and crispy. Cut sandwich in half and serve warm.

Per Serving: Calories: 456; Fat: 24g; Sodium: 961mg; Carbohydrates: 36g; Fiber: 2g; Sugar: 3g; Protein: 19g

Turkey and Avocado Wrap

Prep Time: 5 minutes **Cook Time:** N/A **Serves 1**

Wraps don't have to be complicated to be satisfying. Sometimes a light wrap with simple ingredients energizes you in the middle of a busy day. This recipe uses a fresh avocado, but you can save even more time by purchasing pre-made mashed avocados, sold in individual cups. These aren't the same as guacamole cups, but simply mashed avocado that can be added as a sandwich spread or anywhere you need it. Feel free to customize this wrap to your liking by adding sliced cheese or more vegetables to help fuel your day.

Ingredients

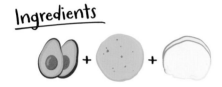

1 small avocado, peeled, halved, pitted, and mashed

1 (10") Mission Sun-Dried Tomato Basil Wrap

2 ounces thinly sliced deli turkey

1 Spread mashed avocado all over wrap in an even layer.

2 Place slices of turkey on top of avocado, slightly overlapping as needed. Begin rolling one side of wrap, tucking in the ends as you go, similar to rolling a burrito.

3 With the seam down, cut wrap in half using a diagonal cut across the center horizontally and serve.

Per Serving: Calories: 503; Fat: 24g; Sodium: 1,117mg; Carbohydrates: 53g; Fiber: 12g; Sugar: 4g; Protein: 18g

Chicken Caesar Salad Wrap

Prep Time: 5 minutes **Cook Time:** N/A **Serves 2**

Take your salads on the go with these fresh wraps. A salad kit gives you all the ingredients you need, from the cheese to the croutons, making this meal possible in less than 5 minutes. Chicken is added for a protein boost and a satisfying taste. This recipe uses pre-cooked chicken, so feel free to use any kind you have on hand such as leftovers, tenders, or rotisserie chicken.

Ingredients

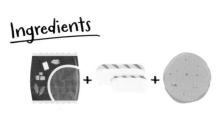

1 (10.6-ounce) package Dole Chopped Caesar Salad Kit

1 (6-ounce) container Oscar Meyer Flame Grilled Chicken Breast Strips, chopped

2 (10") Mission Garden Spinach Herb Wraps

1 Place lettuce and chicken into a large bowl. Open dressing, cheese, and crouton packets and sprinkle on top of salad. Toss to coat.

2 Place half of salad on top of each wrap. Begin rolling one side of wrap, tucking in the ends as you go, similar to rolling a burrito.

3 With the seam down, cut each wrap in half using a diagonal cut across the center horizontally and serve.

Per Serving: Calories: 556; Fat: 27g; Sodium: 1,611mg; Carbohydrates: 48g; Fiber: 6g; Sugar: 5g; Protein: 34g

Tzatziki Chicken Wrap

Prep Time: 5 minutes **Cook Time:** 30 seconds **Serves 1**

Tzatziki is a creamy cucumber and yogurt-based dip that's a staple in Mediterranean cuisine. The dip brings the flavors of this wrap together for a cohesive and satisfying taste throughout. Equally enjoyable cold or lightly toasted, feel free to use this recipe as a base, and dress it up with complementary flavors such as pickled red onion slices, a small handful of diced cucumbers, or a few tablespoons of chopped fresh parsley or other herbs.

Ingredients

1 (7") Papa Pita Greek Pita Flat Bread

3 ounces cold cooked chicken, cubed

2 tablespoons La Terra Fina Tzatziki with Feta Dip & Spread

2 tablespoons crumbled feta cheese

1 Place flatbread on a plate and microwave for 30 seconds.

2 Spread chicken in a line across the center of flatbread. Drizzle tzatziki dip over chicken and sprinkle with feta. Fold the sides of flatbread toward the center to slightly overlap, leaving the top and bottom ends open. Serve.

Per Serving: Calories: 436; Fat: 12g; Sodium: 806mg; Carbohydrates: 41g; Fiber: 4g; Sugar: 4g; Protein: 39g

Sun-Dried Tomato Pesto and Chicken Sandwich

Prep Time: 15 minutes **Cook Time:** 1 minute **Serves 1**

Sun-dried tomato pesto is a simple way to add delicious, concentrated flavor to your meals. It makes a great sandwich spread but can also be added to pasta for a powerful punch of flavor. Paired with fresh creamy mozzarella, it makes the perfect companion for this light and summery sandwich. If you like warm sandwiches, feel free to pop it open-faced into the oven or toaster oven just until the cheese is melted.

Ingredients

1 (3-ounce) Marketside Ciabatta Roll

2 tablespoons Rao's Sundried Tomato Pesto

2 ounces thinly sliced deli roast chicken

1 (1-ounce) slice BelGioioso fresh mozzarella

1 Cut roll in half and place halves into the toaster until golden brown, about 1 minute.

2 Spread pesto onto one half of roll, then layer chicken over pesto. Top with mozzarella. Finally, place the other half of roll on top to complete the sandwich, and serve.

Per Serving: Calories: 415; Fat: 9g; Sodium: 1,375mg; Carbohydrates: 51g; Fiber: 5g; Sugar: 5g; Protein: 24g

Quick and Easy Cheesesteak Sandwiches

Prep Time: 5 minutes **Cook Time:** 10 minutes **Serves 2**

These hefty cheesesteak sandwiches come together quickly for a filling and comforting meal. Piled high with steak, this flavorful dish uses the included packet of seasoning for lots of flavor. (This is definitely ideal for those who haven't yet established a full spice rack!) Feel free to top the sandwich with pepper jack cheese for a spicy kick, or use a couple of tablespoons of warmed Cheez Whiz for a gooey Philly-style alternative.

Ingredients

1 (10.8-ounce) package frozen Gary's QuickSteak Sirloin Beef

½ small yellow onion, sliced

2 (2.5-ounce) Lewis Bake Shop Steak Rolls

4 (1-ounce) slices smoked provolone cheese

1 Warm a nonstick skillet over medium-high heat. Add beef to the skillet and sprinkle with included seasoning packet. Allow beef to cook for 2 minutes, then flip using a spatula.

2 As beef begins to thaw, break it apart with the spatula and add onion. Continue cooking beef and breaking apart as needed for 8 minutes or until no pink remains. When done, beef should be browned, and onion will be softened and lightly caramelized.

3 Divide meat evenly and place it into steak rolls. Top meat with 2 slices of cheese per sandwich and let sandwiches sit for 5 minutes to allow the residual heat from meat to melt cheese. Serve warm.

Per Serving: Calories: 614; Fat: 29g; Sodium: 931mg; Carbohydrates: 39g; Fiber: 1g; Sugar: 6g; Protein: 52g

Tuna Salad Croissant Sandwich

Prep Time: 5 minutes **Cook Time:** N/A **Serves 1**

Bread choice really impacts how much your sandwich is enjoyed. So, soft and buttery croissants are the perfect swap to turn an ordinary sandwich into a more premium-feeling experience. Sink your teeth into the delicious savory tuna salad flavors in this recipe, but if tuna isn't your thing, feel free to use pre-made chicken salad or egg salad.

Ingredients

1 (3-ounce) pouch Starkist Tuna Creations Deli Style Tuna Salad

1 tablespoon dill pickle relish

$\frac{1}{2}$ cup shredded green leaf lettuce

1 medium bakery croissant

1 In a small bowl, mix tuna salad, relish, and lettuce until well combined.

2 Cut croissant in half horizontally. Spread tuna mixture in an even layer on bottom half. Place top half of croissant over tuna salad and serve.

Per Serving: Calories: 329; Fat: 12g; Sodium: 892mg; Carbohydrates: 34g; Fiber: 3g; Sugar: 7g; Protein: 18g

Crispy Chicken Wrap

Prep Time: 5 minutes **Cook Time:** 20 minutes **Serves 1**

Perfect for both lunch and late-night snacks, these Crispy Chicken Wraps are delicious and easy to customize with your favorite sauces. The fusion of honey mustard, barbecue, and ranch tastes great and keeps this go-to meal interesting. For an even bolder flavor, you can use barbecue or lemon pepper–flavored chicken strips, often found next to the plain chicken strips in the frozen section.

Ingredients

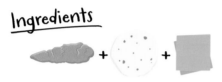

3 ounces frozen Tyson Crispy Chicken Strips

1 (6") flour tortilla

¼ cup shredded sharp Cheddar cheese

1 Preheat the oven to 400°F. Line a baking sheet with parchment paper and place chicken on the sheet. Bake for 20 minutes or until chicken is golden and crispy.

2 Warm a skillet over medium heat. Place tortilla into the skillet and heat for 30 seconds per side.

3 Place warmed tortilla on a large plate and place chicken in the center of tortilla. Sprinkle cheese on top of chicken. Gently fold the sides toward the center, overlapping on top of chicken, leaving ends of tortilla open. Serve warm.

Per Serving: Calories: 413; Fat: 20g; Sodium: 899mg; Carbohydrates: 33g; Fiber: 1g; Sugar: 1g; Protein: 22g

Italian Sub

Prep Time: 5 minutes **Cook Time:** N/A **Serves 1**

Flavorful seasoning transforms a good sandwich into a great sandwich! This classic Italian sub has been elevated by the delicious tastes found in submarine dressing. While you can simply drizzle the dressing on top as a finishing, try tossing some lettuce in the sub dressing for an even punchier bite. For a heartier sandwich, consider layering with a couple more ounces of meat such as Black Forest ham or sandwich-sized pepperoni. For a salad version, ditch the bread, chop the meat and cheese into bite-sized pieces, and add to a bed of chopped romaine lettuce that's coated in submarine dressing.

Ingredients

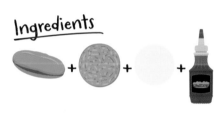

1 (2.5-ounce) Pepperidge Farm Soft White Hoagie Roll with Sesame Seeds

2 (1-ounce) slices thinly sliced Genoa salami

1 (1-ounce) slice provolone cheese

1 tablespoon Beano's Original Submarine Dressing

Place roll on a plate and set top bun to the side. Layer salami and cheese on top of bottom half of hoagie. Drizzle sub dressing over meat and cheese and add top of roll. Cut in half and serve.

Per Serving: Calories: 585; Fat: 37g; Sodium: 1,191mg; Carbohydrates: 37g; Fiber: 2g; Sugar: 3g; Protein: 30g

CHAPTER 5

SOUPS AND SALADS

Soups and salads have some of the freshest ingredients and quickest prep times. They're great separately, but they also make a fantastic combination when you're looking for light nutritious meal ideas. In the cooler months, soups also bring an undeniably comforting warmth to your otherwise cold days.

Both salads and soups are generally easy to prepare, but that doesn't mean they lack in flavor. Even if you're a beginner, you'll quickly learn in the following pages that pre-made salad and canned soup can be easily upgraded to taste more homemade, look like a premium menu item, and serve as a genuinely nice meal. Plus, these recipes won't have you loading up on a cart full of produce or chopping endlessly for a big pot of soup, but they will give you the tools to create some easy staples for every season.

This chapter is loaded with three-ingredient versions of childhood favorites such as Creamy Tomato Soup and Elevated Chicken Noodle Soup, but also contains new and unique recipes such as creamy Avocado Chicken Salad for a flavorful change of pace. Use this chapter to inspire your creativity and perhaps even cement a new understanding that soups and salads can be easy, enjoyable, and exciting.

Tomato Cucumber Salad

Prep Time: 5 minutes **Cook Time:** N/A **Serves 1**

Salad doesn't always have to utilize a bowl of lettuce. This simple salad is perfect as a side dish to pasta, or it can be enjoyed on its own. The fresh crunch of cucumber and juicy vibrant tomatoes are a wonderful combination when paired with the tang of an herb-filled vinaigrette. Add volume to this dish by adding a drained can of chickpeas, slices of red onion, and crumbled feta cheese. Allowing the salad to marinate infuses the flavor of the dressing into the vegetables more fully for a more enjoyable salad. Feel free to add mozzarella pearls for a creamy cheesy addition.

Ingredients

½ cup halved cherry tomatoes

¾ cup diced cucumber

3 tablespoons Kraft Greek Vinaigrette Salad Dressing

Place all ingredients into a medium bowl and toss to combine. Cover the bowl with plastic wrap and refrigerate for at least 30 minutes to allow vegetables to marinate fully. Serve chilled.

Per Serving: Calories: 99; Fat: 8g; Sodium: 544mg; Carbohydrates: 9g; Fiber: 1g; Sugar: 4g; Protein: 1g

Pasta Salad

Prep Time: 10 minutes **Cook Time:** 3 minutes **Serves 2**

This easy three-ingredient pasta salad is so simple—you don't even have to boil noodles. This recipe uses pre-cooked pasta to save you lots of time.

Ingredients

1 (7-ounce) package Barilla Ready Pasta Rotini

1 cup quartered cherry tomatoes

4 ounces mozzarella cheese pearls

1 Empty package of pasta into a skillet over medium heat. Warm for 3 minutes, stirring occasionally, then place into a medium bowl and allow to cool for 10 minutes.

2 Toss pasta with cherry tomatoes and mozzarella pearls and serve.

Per Serving: Calories: 311; Fat: 11g; Sodium: 357mg; Carbohydrates: 38g; Fiber: 5g; Sugar: 2g; Protein: 17g

Creamy Tomato Soup

Prep Time: 5 minutes **Cook Time:** 22 minutes **Makes 4 cups** (serving size: 1 cup)

Tomato soup is savory, creamy, and a total comfort food. If you're looking for a complement to Chapter 4's Tuna Melt, this easy soup is just the thing!

Ingredients

1 (28-ounce) can San Marzano Peeled Tomatoes

¼ teaspoon salt

2 cups vegetable broth

½ cup heavy cream

1 Place all ingredients into a blender and purée until smooth, about 45 seconds.

2 Pour mixture into a soup pot or medium saucepan and bring to a boil over high heat, for about 7 minutes. Reduce to a simmer for 15 minutes or until soup is thick and deep red. Serve warm.

Per Serving: Calories: 165; Fat: 10g; Sodium: 764mg; Carbohydrates: 15g; Fiber: 3g; Sugar: 9g; Protein: 2g

Avocado Chicken Salad

Prep Time: 5 minutes **Cook Time:** N/A **Serves 1**

This ultra-creamy twist on traditional chicken salad doesn't use mayonnaise. Instead, mashed avocado is used for a green-hued salad that's big on flavor. Avocado browns quickly once cut into, so it's best to make this right before you plan to eat it, and don't skip the lime—acidity helps prevent browning. Enjoy this meal on a tostada, with crackers, inside a wrap, or with a fork.

Ingredients

1 small avocado, peeled, halved, and pitted

¼ teaspoon salt

⅛ teaspoon ground black pepper

Juice of ½ small lime

1 cup cold diced cooked chicken breast

1 Scoop avocado halves out into a medium bowl and mash until mostly smooth.

2 Sprinkle salt and pepper on top of mashed avocado and pour in lime juice. Mix until combined.

3 Gently stir in chicken until well coated and serve.

Per Serving: Calories: 472; Fat: 24g; Sodium: 698mg; Carbohydrates: 13g; Fiber: 9g; Sugar: 1g; Protein: 46g

Tortellini and Kale Soup

Prep Time: 5 minutes **Cook Time:** 15 minutes **Serves 2**

This broth-based soup is ideal for cold days. Each bite of soft tortellini bursts with savory cheese flavor that goes well with the earthiness of the kale. Whether you're not feeling well, or simply need something comforting to warm you up after a cold walk home, this quick soup is the perfect choice. This is a great recipe to use extra chopped vegetables sitting in your refrigerator, such as mushrooms, onions, or carrots. Simply add a tablespoon of oil to the pot and sauté the vegetables until tender, then follow the recipe directions from there.

Ingredients

4 cups chicken broth

1 cup fresh chopped kale, firmly packed

2 cups frozen Louisa Four Cheese Tortellini

1 In a soup pot or medium saucepan, bring chicken broth to a boil over high heat. Add kale and reduce heat to medium. Simmer for 7 minutes or until kale is tender and wilted.

2 Add tortellini and cook for 3 minutes. When done, tortellini will look slightly puffy and soft. Serve warm.

Per Serving: Calories: 353; Fat: 8g; Sodium: 2,390mg; Carbohydrates: 48g; Fiber: 2g; Sugar: 4g; Protein: 20g

Butternut Squash Soup

Prep Time: 5 minutes **Cook Time:** 11 minutes **Serves 2**

Savor all the deliciousness of fall-inspired soup without the hassle of cutting and roasting a butternut squash. This recipe uses frozen squash cubes for a thick and creamy soup that's accented with a sweet splash of coconut milk. It's perfect for chilly days and can be made in advance for those who like to do their cooking at the beginning of the week. Try adding a pinch of nutmeg for a deep, warm, spicy addition.

Ingredients

1 (10-ounce) bag frozen microwavable butternut squash cubes

3 cups vegetable broth

¼ teaspoon salt

⅛ teaspoon ground black pepper

2 tablespoons coconut milk

1 Following package instructions, gently massage bag of frozen squash to break up any clumps. Place bag into the microwave and cook for 6 minutes. Allow bag to stand for 1 minute before opening.

2 Add entire bag of squash cubes to a blender and add broth, salt, and pepper. Blend on high for 30 seconds or until completely smooth.

3 Pour mixture into a medium saucepan and cook for 5 minutes over medium heat. To serve, separate into two servings and drizzle the top of each with 1 tablespoon coconut milk.

Per Serving: Calories: 125; Fat: 3g; Sodium: 1,494mg; Carbohydrates: 24g; Fiber: 2g; Sugar: 7g; Protein: 3g

Cheesy Potato Soup

Prep Time: 5 minutes **Cook Time:** 20 minutes **Makes 4 cups** (serving size: 1 cup)

Potato soup is a warm comfort in a bowl! Modify this delicious recipe by adding a spoonful of sour cream or cooked, chopped bacon. This recipe makes a big batch and freezes well, so you can meal prep it. To freeze the soup, portion it out as desired and place it into freezer-safe zip-top bags. Lay them flat in your freezer for easy defrosting. When you want the soup, place one of the bags into the refrigerator overnight or submerge it into cool water for 20 minutes or until thawed. Then microwave soup for 3 minutes, stirring halfway through.

1 (10.5-ounce) can Campbell's Cheddar Cheese Soup

1 cup water

1 (2.75-ounce) packet Pioneer Peppered Gravy Mix

2 cups frozen Ore-Ida Potatoes O'Brien with Onions & Peppers

1 Warm a soup pot or medium saucepan over medium heat. Add soup, water, and gravy mix, and then whisk to combine. Bring mixture to a boil, for about 2 minutes.

2 Add frozen potatoes, reduce the heat to a simmer, and continue cooking for 18 minutes. Potatoes should be tender, and soup should be thick. Serve warm.

Per Serving: Calories: 190; Fat: 7g; Sodium: 972mg; Carbohydrates: 29g; Fiber: 2g; Sugar: 5g; Protein: 2g

Spinach, Apple, and Pecan Salad

Prep Time: 5 minutes **Cook Time:** N/A **Serves 1**

This light and fresh-tasting salad is as full of nutrients as it is loaded with flavor. To bring the delectable taste to the next level, explore different finishing options: poppyseed dressing, raspberry vinaigrette, or a simple spritz of fresh lemon juice. Add grilled chicken slices or diced rotisserie chicken for a protein boost that will leave you full and satisfied between meals.

Ingredients

2 cups fresh baby spinach, loosely packed

1 medium honey crisp apple, cored and diced

¼ cup chopped roasted pecans

Place spinach into a serving bowl. Top with apple and toss lightly with two forks to combine. Sprinkle pecans across the top of salad and serve.

Per Serving: Calories: 299; Fat: 19g; Sodium: 48mg; Carbohydrates: 29g; Fiber: 8g; Sugar: 19g; Protein: 5g

Elevated Chicken Noodle Soup

Prep Time: 5 minutes **Cook Time:** 8 minutes **Serves 2**

Whether it's a sick day or just a cold one, a hot bowl of chicken noodle soup can't be beat. And, yes, fully homemade soup is delicious, but it usually requires a myriad of ingredients that you're unlikely to have on hand and requires lots of chopping. Canned soup is a convenient alternative that, with a couple of additions, will have you savoring its comforting warmth in no time. For a spicy kick, try this soup with a sprinkle of crushed red pepper flakes.

Ingredients

1 (18.6-ounce) can Campbell's Chunky Classic Chicken Noodle Soup

3 tablespoons chopped fresh parsley

2 tablespoons fresh lemon juice

1 In a medium saucepan over medium heat, warm soup until heated through, stirring occasionally, for about 8 minutes.

2 Stir in parsley and remove soup from the heat. Separate soup into two bowls for serving. Add 1 tablespoon lemon juice to each bowl and stir to combine. Serve warm.

Per Serving: Calories: 128; Fat: 1g; Sodium: 859mg; Carbohydrates: 16g; Fiber: 3g; Sugar: 2g; Protein: 9g

Spicy Ramen Soup

Prep Time: 5 minutes **Cook Time:** 3 minutes **Serves 1**

There's hardly a more classic college dish than ramen noodles, but the days of preparing them with one-note flavors are long gone. This simple yet elevated soup introduces a wonderful umami addition, soy sauce, for a strong savory element. Plus, just the right amount of spice from sriracha complements the ramen's chicken flavor. Feel free to sprinkle in a fresh ingredient such as chopped cilantro, or add some fried wonton strips for a bit of crunch.

Ingredients

2 cups water

1 (3-ounce) package Nissin Top Ramen Chicken Flavor

2 tablespoons soy sauce

1 tablespoon sriracha

1 Follow package instructions: Bring water to a boil in a medium saucepan over medium heat. Add dry noodles to the pan and cook for 3 minutes, stirring occasionally.

2 When done, noodles should be tender. Stir in packet of included seasoning and soy sauce. Stir in sriracha. Serve warm.

Per Serving: Calories: 411; Fat: 14g; Sodium: 3,647mg; Carbohydrates: 58g; Fiber: 2g; Sugar: 3g; Protein: 12g

Avocado Black Bean Salad

Prep Time: 5 minutes **Cook Time:** N/A **Serves 1**

This Southwest-inspired salad is filled with healthy fats and protein to keep you full throughout your day. Enjoy it with a spoon, or scoop it up with lime tortilla chips for a salty crunch. Add a squeeze of lime juice or a tablespoon of chopped fresh cilantro to boost the flavor before you dig in. This salad can be enjoyed alone, in a warmed corn tortilla, or as part of a meal alongside seared steak and a steamed bag of rice.

Ingredients

½ medium avocado, peeled, pitted, and diced

½ cup canned black beans, drained and rinsed

¼ cup canned corn, drained

¼ teaspoon salt

Mix all ingredients in a small bowl until well combined. Serve.

Per Serving: Calories: 249; Fat: 10g; Sodium: 918mg; Carbohydrates: 31g; Fiber: 13g; Sugar: 0g; Protein: 9g

Cranberry Pecan Chicken Salad

Prep Time: 5 minutes **Cook Time:** N/A **Serves 2**

Sweet and crunchy, this chicken salad is perfect for lunch. It can be enjoyed in a croissant, alongside crackers, or in the low-carb embrace of a crisp lettuce wrap. Salad toppers are found in the condiment aisle near the croutons, and they make for an excellent, delectable shortcut. No chopping is required because these toppers already come in small pieces. While you can eat this chicken salad right away, leaving it in the refrigerator for a couple hours will allow the flavors to intertwine for a more developed and cohesive result. Plus, it will also soften the ingredients for a more enjoyable chew.

Ingredients

1 (12.5-ounce) can chunk chicken breast in water, drained

1/2 cup mayonnaise

1/4 cup sweetened dried cranberries and candied pecans salad topper

1/4 teaspoon ground black pepper

1 Place chicken on a cutting board. Chop chicken into 1/2"-thick pieces and place into a medium bowl.

2 Add mayonnaise, salad topper bits, and pepper to the bowl and stir until well combined. All chicken should be coated in mayonnaise. Serve. Store leftovers in an airtight container in the refrigerator for up to 3 days.

Per Serving: Calories: 604; Fat: 49g; Sodium: 1,039mg; Carbohydrates: 10g; Fiber: 2g; Sugar: 7g; Protein: 28g

Lemon and Parmesan Kale Salad

Prep Time: 5 minutes **Cook Time:** N/A **Serves 1**

Kale is nutrient-dense and rich in fiber, making it an ideal base for salad. This simple salad is bright with a sharp, nutty flavor from the Parmesan. It's perfect as an entrée, but it can be halved for a healthy side dish that pairs with chicken, steak, or salmon. You can use leftover kale in smoothies or toss a handful in your next soup for an extra nutrient boost.

Ingredients

2 cups fresh chopped kale

2 tablespoons Marzetti Simply Lemon Vinaigrette Dressing & Marinade

2 tablespoons fresh grated Parmesan cheese

1 Place kale into a large bowl and gently massage leaves for 30 seconds to remove bitterness. Rinse kale and pat dry with a paper towel. Then, place kale into a serving bowl.

2 Pour dressing on top of kale and toss with two forks to coat. Sprinkle Parmesan on top and serve.

Per Serving: Calories: 107; Fat: 8g; Sodium: 442mg; Carbohydrates: 6g; Fiber: 1g; Sugar: 2g; Protein: 4g

CHAPTER 6

CHICKEN AND SEAFOOD MAIN DISHES

Chicken is one of the world's most popular proteins, and it offers a range of versatile and delicious meals that are both simple to make and good for you. In college, your access to raw chicken might be limited. While this chapter gives some easy recipes that start from scratch, it also features plenty of shortcuts that allow you to upgrade store-bought options to make them taste homemade. Whenever possible, this book uses simple, cost-effective cuts of meat that are boneless, skinless, and don't require extensive processing or cutting.

Seafood has a reputation for being notoriously difficult to cook, but it has excellent nutritional benefits, making it worth the time to learn how to make easy seafood dishes from your kitchen. You'll learn to utilize a variety of seafood and turn even the simplest of grocery store finds into a meal with just a few additional ingredients. By scaling down the food you're cooking with while simultaneously boosting the flavor, this chapter will foster a love of cooking small-batch seafood meals.

This combination seafood and chicken chapter will keep you coming back for more! With recipes like Spicy Glazed Salmon and Bacon-Wrapped Chicken Tenderloins, get ready to dive into a sea of exciting dishes that will make over your meal time.

Southwest Power Bowl

Prep Time: 5 minutes **Cook Time:** 8 minutes **Serves 2**

Bowl meals that blend cold and warm ingredients give you the crunch of a salad with the comfort of a warm dish. This recipe uses a Southwest-style blend of rice, beans, and vegetables for a satisfying meal you can whip up in less than 15 minutes. If you're packing this for lunch, keep the lettuce in a sealable bag and add it after reheating the chicken and vegetables. To punch up the flavor, feel free to add your favorite sauces such as salsa, sour cream, or a cilantro lime sauce.

Ingredients

1 (12.7-ounce) bag frozen Birds Eye Southwest Style Power Blend

4 ounces cooked chicken breast, cut into bite-sized pieces

4 cups chopped romaine lettuce

1 Follow package instructions to heat Power Blend in the microwave and set aside.

2 Place chicken into a medium microwave-safe bowl and microwave for 1 minute or until heated through.

3 Divide lettuce evenly between two medium bowls. Top with chicken and Power Blend. Serve warm.

4 If keeping the second serving for leftovers, store chicken, Power Blend, and lettuce separately.

Per Serving: Calories: 303; Fat: 4g; Sodium: 235mg; Carbohydrates: 38g; Fiber: 10g; Sugar: 6g; Protein: 28g

Chicken Fajita Rice Bowl

Prep Time: 5 minutes **Cook Time:** 15 minutes **Serves 2**

Bowl meals are popular because they're simple and don't take much effort. This recipe uses pantry and frozen ingredients to make a delicious savory fajita bowl. These are ingredients you can keep in your pantry and freezer for months and grab them when you need something fast. This dish reheats well and can be dressed up to your liking with shredded cheese, pickled jalapeños, sour cream, and/or guacamole. To reheat, warm in the microwave for 1½–2 minutes or until heated through, stirring halfway through cooking time.

Ingredients

1 (8.8-ounce) microwave pouch Spanish-style rice

¼ cup water

1 cup frozen Birds Eye Tri-Colored Pepper & Onion Medley

1 (6-ounce) package John Soules Foods Chicken Fajitas Strips

1 Cook rice according to package instructions and set aside.

2 Add water to a skillet over medium heat, then add vegetables and chicken pieces. Cover with a lid for 3 minutes, then remove lid and stir. Leave the lid off to continue cooking down water as vegetables soften, about 7 minutes. Once vegetables have softened and chicken is heated through, add rice to the skillet and mix all ingredients to combine. Serve warm.

Per Serving: Calories: 305; Fat: 5g; Sodium: 768mg; Carbohydrates: 38g; Fiber: 2g; Sugar: 5g; Protein: 23g

Barbecue Chicken–Stuffed Sweet Potato

Prep Time: 5 minutes **Cook Time:** 7 minutes **Serves 1**

There's nothing like a comforting barbecue meal. This dish blends the health benefits and taste of a sweet potato with smoky barbecue sauce for a balanced and delicious dish that won't take long to make. This comforting dish has tender, savory chicken in each bite. It's perfect for warming you up on a cold day and can even be scaled to make a batch for the week. Feel free to use pulled pork or unseasoned shredded meat if you prefer.

Ingredients

1 medium sweet potato

½ cup Lloyd's Seasoned Shredded Chicken in Original BBQ Sauce

2 tablespoons chopped green onions

1 Use a fork to pierce sweet potato about eight times all over, to allow steam to escape. Place potato on a medium microwave-safe plate and into the microwave. Cook for 5 minutes or until potato is steaming and a fork easily goes in. If potato is not tender enough, cook for additional 30-second increments until tender.

2 Cut potato open in half lengthwise as you would a traditional baked potato.

3 Place chicken into a medium microwave-safe bowl and then into the microwave. Cook for 2 minutes, stirring halfway through cooking time. Place warmed chicken into the center of sweet potato and sprinkle chicken with green onions. Serve warm.

Per Serving: Calories: 294; Fat: 6g; Sodium: 1,032mg; Carbohydrates: 45g; Fiber: 4g; Sugar: 24g; Protein: 14g

Tuna Sushi Bowl

Prep Time: 5 minutes **Cook Time:** 2 minutes **Serves 1**

Sushi rolls are delicious, but they take a lot of time and technique to master. This recipe delivers all the flavors of a tuna roll but comes without the extra steps. Microwaved sticky rice is a major time saver, allowing you to enjoy this meal in minutes. Feel free to elevate the flavors in this dish with a splash of soy sauce, dash of sriracha mayonnaise, or a few tablespoons of chopped cucumber for a fresh crunch.

Ingredients

1 (7.4-ounce) Annie Chun's Sticky White Rice Bowl

1 (2.5-ounce) pouch Bumblebee Lemon Sesame & Ginger Seasoned Tuna

1 (0.35-ounce) package Annie Chun's Organic Seaweed Snacks

1 Follow package instructions to heat rice bowl in the microwave. Use a fork to fluff rice.

2 Open tuna pouch and mix with a fork while it's still in the package to break up any large pieces. Place tuna on top of rice.

3 Serve with seaweed pieces to scoop up rice and tuna.

Per Serving: Calories: 447; Fat: 6g; Sodium: 497mg; Carbohydrates: 76g; Fiber: 3g; Sugar: 2g; Protein: 23g

Spicy Glazed Salmon

Prep Time: 5 minutes **Cook Time:** 12 minutes **Serves 1**

Salmon is a healthy protein choice that's easy to cook. Hot honey, which is infused with chili peppers, and soy sauce combine in this recipe for a savory and spicy sauce, transforming into a gorgeous glaze once cooked. When choosing salmon, be sure to look for fresh pieces that don't smell overly fishy, and be mindful of when you purchase it, because it should only sit in the refrigerator for a maximum of two days. Wild-caught salmon is darker red and tends to be more expensive, while light pink farm-raised salmon with prominent white streaks typically costs much less. Bags of frozen salmon are also budget-friendly; just be sure to follow the package directions for thawing before you begin cooking.

Ingredients

1 (6-ounce) salmon filet, skin removed

1 tablespoon hot honey

1 tablespoon soy sauce

¼ teaspoon salt

1 Preheat the oven to 375°F. Line a baking sheet with parchment paper and place salmon on the parchment.

2 In a small bowl, whisk together hot honey and soy sauce. Brush salmon all over generously with honey mixture. Sprinkle each side with salt.

3 Place salmon into the oven and bake for 12 minutes or until the internal temperature reaches 145°F and salmon flakes easily. When done the edges will be dark brown from caramelized honey. Serve warm.

Per Serving: Calories: 424; Fat: 18g; Sodium: 1,559mg; Carbohydrates: 18g; Fiber: 0g; Sugar: 17g; Protein: 36g

Bacon-Wrapped Chicken Tenderloins

Prep Time: 10 minutes **Cook Time:** 15 minutes **Serves 2**

Smoky and sweet, these chicken tenders are an easy weeknight dinner or game-day eat. Crispy bacon and tender juicy chicken make them an excellent entrée that goes with all your favorite barbecue-style sides such as potato salad and mac and cheese, or alongside lighter options like an easy garden salad.

Ingredients

4 (2-ounce) chicken tenderloins

¼ teaspoon salt

¼ cup barbecue sauce

4 slices bacon

1 Preheat the oven to 400°F. Line a baking sheet with parchment paper and set aside.

2 Sprinkle chicken tenderloins with salt. Brush tenderloins all over with barbecue sauce.

3 Wrap one slice bacon around each tenderloin as evenly as possible and secure with toothpicks. Place tenderloins on the prepared baking sheet and into the oven. Bake for 15 minutes, turning over when 5 minutes of cook time remain to ensure that bacon is evenly crisped. When done, chicken tenderloin should have an internal temperature of 165°F and bacon should be crispy and browned. Serve warm.

Per Serving: Calories: 173; Fat: 6g; Sodium: 1,038mg; Carbohydrates: 15g; Fiber: 0g; Sugar: 12g; Protein: 11g

Spicy Chicken Potstickers

Prep Time: 5 minutes **Cook Time:** 12 minutes **Serves 2**

Made with crushed dried chilies, oil, garlic, onions, and more, chili crisp is the multiuse condiment you didn't know you needed. Whether topping your potstickers or adding a spoonful of spice to your morning eggs, this textured condiment easily earns itself a spot in the spice cabinet. This recipe makes a light sauce that coats the soft potstickers and creates an irresistible dish. Try topping with sliced green onions for a vibrant fresh taste.

Ingredients

⅓ cup chicken broth

10 frozen Tai Pei Chicken Potstickers (plus 2 tablespoons of included sauce)

1 tablespoon chili crisp

1 Pour chicken broth into a skillet over medium-high heat. Add potstickers in a single layer and drizzle with sauce. Bring to a boil, then cover and reduce heat to medium-low. Simmer for 8 minutes or until potstickers are softened and have an internal temperature of 165°F.

2 Uncover and continue simmering for 2 minutes or until most of the liquid evaporates. Top with chili crisp and serve.

Per Serving: Calories: 314; Fat: 11g; Sodium: 1,373mg; Carbohydrates: 40g; Fiber: 3g; Sugar: 9g; Protein: 13g

Skillet Salsa Chicken

Prep Time: 5 minutes **Cook Time:** 15 minutes **Serves 2**

This recipe will open your eyes to just how boldly impactful chicken dishes can be with only a handful of ingredients. To explore different flavor profiles, you can swap in zingy salsa verde or chunky black bean salsa. And to make it a meal, you can shred up the chicken and serve it on top of microwaved rice or rolled up in a flour tortilla. If you like to meal prep, consider doubling this recipe and using containers to create taco bowls for each day of the week. Fill them with your choice of toppings for an easy microwave-friendly dish ready any time.

Ingredients

4 (2-ounce) chicken tenderloins

2 tablespoons taco seasoning

1 cup mild salsa

1/4 cup water

1 Warm a skillet over medium heat. Place chicken on large plate. Sprinkle taco seasoning to completely coat each piece of chicken on both sides. Place chicken into the skillet and pour salsa on top.

2 Pour water onto the side of the skillet, avoiding washing seasoning off of chicken. Bring to a boil and then reduce to a simmer and cover. Cook for 15 minutes or until the internal temperature of chicken is at least 165°F. When done, chicken will be tender and juicy. Shred with two forks, stir, and serve.

Per Serving: Calories: 83; Fat: 0g; Sodium: 1,561mg; Carbohydrates: 13g; Fiber: 5g; Sugar: 9g; Protein: 6g

Teriyaki Chicken Thighs

Prep Time: 5 minutes **Cook Time:** 15 minutes **Serves 2**

Chicken thighs are a very flavorful cut of meat and don't require a lot of prep. Adding teriyaki sauce is a simple way to make a takeout-style dish with a fraction of the time and cost. Add a package of microwave-steamed rice and your favorite steamed vegetables such as broccoli florets for a satisfying meal that you can feel proud of cooking in your own kitchen. If you don't have any teriyaki sauce on hand but you have soy sauce in the pantry, you can make your own teriyaki sauce by mixing ¼ cup of soy sauce with equal amounts brown sugar.

Ingredients

1 tablespoon vegetable oil

2 (4-ounce) boneless skinless chicken thighs

½ teaspoon salt

¼ cup Panda Express Chinese Kitchen Mandarin Teriyaki Sauce

1 Warm vegetable oil in a skillet over medium heat, for about 2 minutes. Sprinkle chicken thighs on both sides with salt. Place chicken into the skillet and sear on each side for 4 minutes.

2 Pour teriyaki into the skillet on top of chicken and flip chicken so each side is well coated. Reduce the heat to a simmer and cook for 5 minutes, turning and rotating chicken occasionally.

3 When done, sauce in the skillet should be thickened and coat chicken in a shiny glaze. The internal temperature of chicken should be at least 165°F and juices run clear. Let stand for 5 minutes, then serve warm with any remaining pan sauce.

Per Serving: Calories: 400; Fat: 22g; Sodium: 1,189mg; Carbohydrates: 16g; Fiber: 0g; Sugar: 14g; Protein: 28g

Baked Ranch Chicken Breast

Prep Time: 5 minutes **Cook Time:** 25 minutes **Serves 2**

Dry ranch dressing mix is a great way to pack in a lot of flavor at once. It's pantry-friendly and filled with savory herb flavor. Chicken breast doesn't have a lot of fat and can easily dry out in the oven. The mayonnaise adds fat, ensuring that the chicken stays juicy during cooking and doesn't leave you with a dry and chewy cut of meat. Alternatively, you can use a drizzle of olive oil. Pair this dish with a steamer bag of broccoli and a microwave cup of mashed potatoes for a complete meal in less than 30 minutes.

Ingredients

2 tablespoons mayonnaise

2 (6-ounce) boneless skinless chicken breasts

¼ cup dry ranch seasoning mix

1 Preheat the oven to 400°F. Line a baking sheet with parchment paper and set aside.

2 Use a spoon to spread mayonnaise on all sides of chicken. Generously sprinkle dry ranch mixture onto chicken and pat it gently to adhere to mayonnaise.

3 Place chicken on the baking sheet and into the oven. Bake for 25 minutes or until the internal temperature is at least 165°F and the juices from chicken run clear. Serve warm.

Per Serving: Calories: 249; Fat: 12g; Sodium: 1,740mg; Carbohydrates: 12g; Fiber: 0g; Sugar: 0g; Protein: 20g

Garlic Butter Shrimp

Prep Time: 5 minutes **Cook Time:** 5 minutes **Serves 2**

If you're new to cooking raw shrimp, understand that this recipe specifically calls for the shelled and deveined variety. That means the shells are already removed and so is the shrimp's intestinal tract, the small dark line that runs on the underside of the shrimp's body. The shrimp is still raw, however, so it should appear gray, not pink as it does when fully cooked. With the hard work already done for you, this dish comes together in just minutes, right in your skillet. Feel free to finish with a squeeze of fresh lemon juice!

Ingredients

3 tablespoons salted butter

6 ounces uncooked medium shrimp, shelled and deveined

½ teaspoon salt

2 cloves garlic, peeled and finely minced

1 Melt butter in a skillet over medium heat. Place shrimp into the skillet and sprinkle with salt. Sauté shrimp for 2 minutes per side.

2 Stir in garlic and cook for an additional minute. When done, shrimp should be opaque, pink, and slightly curled into a C shape. The internal temperature should be at least 145°F. Serve warm with remaining drippings from the pan spooned on top.

Per Serving: Calories: 216; Fat: 17g; Sodium: 1,199mg; Carbohydrates: 2g; Fiber: 0g; Sugar: 0g; Protein: 12g

Salmon Patties

Prep Time: 5 minutes **Cook Time:** 8 minutes **Serves 1**

Crisp on the outside while soft and juicy inside, these mouthwatering salmon patties are ready in less than 15 minutes. Choosing flavored salmon pouches for seasoning is perfect for those who don't have a large spice collection. This recipe uses a lemon and chive variety for a fresh flavor, but feel free to explore all the options and choose one that speaks to you. Enjoy alongside a fresh salad or steamed rice for a protein-packed filling meal.

Ingredients

2 (2.5-ounce) pouches Chicken of the Sea Wild-Caught Pink Salmon with Lemon & Chive

3 tablespoons mayonnaise

¼ cup plain panko breadcrumbs

1 Warm a nonstick skillet over medium heat. Place salmon in a medium bowl and use a fork to flake it apart. Add mayonnaise and breadcrumbs, then mix together until well combined.

2 Form salmon mixture into two (4"-wide) patties. Place patties into the skillet and cook for 4 minutes per side, or until golden brown. Remove patties from the skillet and allow them to cool for 5 minutes before serving.

Per Serving: Calories: 522; Fat: 33g; Sodium: 985mg; Carbohydrates: 24g; Fiber: 0g; Sugar: 3g; Protein: 30g

Spicy Blackened Shrimp

Prep Time: 5 minutes **Cook Time:** 8 minutes **Serves 2**

If you're a fan of spice, this recipe is sure to be one of your new favorite go-to options. Blackened seasoning is made from a bold blend of spices such as paprika, celery seed, and red pepper. It tases delicious on both chicken and shrimp, making this a versatile seasoning for your spice rack. Make it a meal by serving it over Creamy Fettuccine Alfredo with Broccoli (Chapter 8); the complementary creamy pasta will cool down the spices just a bit and fill you up with comforting flavor. Or, Knorr Pasta Sides in Alfredo flavor is a convenient alternative option for a quick and easy-to-make side dish.

Ingredients

6 ounces uncooked large shrimp, shelled and deveined

2 tablespoons olive oil

1 teaspoon Old Bay Blackened Seasoning

1 Place shrimp into a medium bowl and drizzle with olive oil. Sprinkle with blackened seasoning and toss to fully coat.

2 Warm a nonstick skillet over medium heat and then add shrimp. Cook 4 minutes per side or until the internal temperature is at least 145°F and shrimp become opaque pink. When done, shrimp should have a dark brown crust from seasoning and curl into a C shape. Serve warm.

Per Serving: Calories: 179; Fat: 14g; Sodium: 571mg; Carbohydrates: 1g; Fiber: 0g; Sugar: 0g; Protein: 12g

CHAPTER 7

BEEF AND PORK MAIN DISHES

There are many delicious meal options that come from beef and pork ingredients! The meaty marvels you'll find in this chapter are full entrées that are packed with protein and flavor. Better yet, each was specifically designed to be quickly prepared in a small cooking space with easy-to-access tools, and no fancy gadgets.

This chapter will show you how to take a list of simple meal ideas and create them in no time. Plus, it's food you'll actually want to eat—and food that can easily be prepared in a couple batches if you're eager to cook for friends. The best part is that these dishes are easy to flavor, customizable to fit your taste preferences, and of course, completely delicious. This chapter covers everything from game-day eats to weeknight dishes that you can put in your weekly rotation. There's even something for those special occasions when you want to make a more elegant dish, such as Pan-Seared Strip Steak.

From nostalgic One Pot Spaghetti to Chili Cheese Fries and Steak and Noodle Stir-Fry, this chapter has no shortage of awesome beef and pork main dishes to add some flavor to your day.

One Pot Spaghetti

Prep Time: 5 minutes **Cook Time:** 25 minutes **Serves 2**

This recipe is purely satisfying comfort food at its best: warm, nostalgic, and almost effortless, so you can enjoy it faster. Cooking the spaghetti directly in the sauce allows the pasta to absorb all the classic bold flavor. For even more flavor, serve with a side of garlic bread. And in the same way that spaghetti tends to taste better the next day, this dish makes for a delicious leftover meal as well. Simply sprinkle a tablespoon of water on top and heat it for 2 minutes in the microwave, then stir and enjoy.

Ingredients

⅓ pound 80/20 ground beef

2 cups pasta sauce

½ teaspoon salt

1 cup water

4 ounces dry pot-size spaghetti

1 In a medium saucepan over medium heat, brown ground beef until no pink remains, about 7 minutes. Drain any grease and return the pan to the burner.

2 Stir in pasta sauce, salt, and water. Add spaghetti, pressing down gently to ensure it's submerged. Increase heat to high.

3 Bring to a boil, then reduce heat to medium-low. Simmer, stirring occasionally, for 15 minutes or until spaghetti is tender. Serve warm.

4 Store leftovers in an airtight container in the refrigerator for up to 4 days.

Per Serving: Calories: 479; Fat: 11g; Sodium: 1,731mg; Carbohydrates: 63g; Fiber: 7g; Sugar: 15g; Protein: 25g

Cauliflower Rice and Beef Skillet

Prep Time: 5 minutes **Cook Time:** 12 minutes **Serves 2**

This low-carb meal is filling, packed with flavor, and a sneaky way to get your vegetables in for the day. As the cauliflower absorbs the flavors of the salsa, it loses its prominent taste and blends into a cohesive dish. This recipe uses ground beef, but you can also use ground turkey, ground chicken, or cooked shredded chicken. Opt for meatless crumbles for a vegetarian twist.

Ingredients

1/2 pound 80/20 ground beef

1 (10-ounce) bag frozen Birds Eye Steamfresh Riced Cauliflower

1/2 teaspoon salt

1/4 teaspoon ground black pepper

1 1/2 cups chunky salsa

1 In a skillet over medium heat, brown ground beef until no pink remains, about 7 minutes.

2 While beef is cooking, follow package instructions to steam cauliflower in the microwave and set aside.

3 Once beef is done, drain any grease and return skillet to the burner, still on medium heat. Stir salt, pepper, cauliflower, and salsa into the skillet. Mix together until well combined and cook for 5 minutes or until cauliflower has reddened from soaking up some salsa. Serve warm.

Per Serving: Calories: 273; Fat: 10g; Sodium: 2,050mg; Carbohydrates: 19g; Fiber: 9g; Sugar: 12g; Protein: 21g

Honey Mustard Pork Chop

Prep Time: 5 minutes **Cook Time:** 12 minutes **Serves 1**

With its sweet and tangy flavor profile, honey mustard is the perfect partner for pork. This sauce complements the mild taste of the pork chop and aids in creating a beautiful caramelization on the exterior. Pork chops can be a great budget-friendly meal, especially when you're craving something meaty. This dish also easily pairs with a wide variety of side dishes from mac and cheese to mashed potatoes.

Ingredients

¼ teaspoon salt

⅛ teaspoon ground black pepper

1 tablespoon honey

1½ teaspoons Dijon mustard

1 (6-ounce) boneless pork chop

1 Spray a skillet with nonstick cooking spray and warm over medium heat.

2 In a small bowl, mix salt, pepper, honey, and mustard until combined. Generously spread mustard mixture over both sides of pork chop.

3 Place pork chop into the preheated skillet to sear each side, about 2 minutes per side. Use tongs to flip pork chop over.

4 Reduce the heat to medium-low, and continue cooking pork chop, about 4 minutes per side, until the internal temperature is at least 145°F. When done, the center should be lightly pink, and the edges should be browned. Serve warm.

Per Serving: Calories: 293; Fat: 6g; Sodium: 841mg; Carbohydrates: 19g; Fiber: 0g; Sugar: 17g; Protein: 34g

Steak and Noodle Stir-Fry

Prep Time: 5 minutes **Cook Time:** 15 minutes **Serves 2**

Whip up this easy stir-fry with the help of a frozen bag of premixed noodles and vegetables. Stir-fries are a super simple and nutritious meal option that tends to highlight Asian flavors to make the tastiest one pot meals. Tender seared steak is the star of this dish, and it cooks very quickly due to its thin slicing. Thinly sliced steak is usually available at the grocery store near cuts of steak but can sometimes be found in the freshly made convenient meals area. This savory vegetable-filled meal comes together in about 20 minutes, making it the perfect full-flavored weeknight dish.

Ingredients

½ pound thinly sliced sirloin steak

¼ teaspoon salt

¼ teaspoon ground black pepper

3 cups frozen Birds Eye Teriyaki Stir-Fry Noodles, Veggies & Sauce

3 tablespoons soy sauce

¼ cup water

1 In a nonstick skillet over medium-high heat, cook steak for about 5 minutes or until no pink remains. Season with salt and pepper. Add vegetable mix, soy sauce, and water to the skillet.

2 Reduce heat to medium and cook for 10 minutes, stirring occasionally until the vegetables are tender. Serve warm.

Per Serving: Calories: 388; Fat: 13g; Sodium: 2,212mg; Carbohydrates: 30g; Fiber: 3g; Sugar: 9g; Protein: 31g

Pizza Quesadilla

Prep Time: 5 minutes **Cook Time:** 6 minutes **Serves 1**

Pizza is a definite staple during college life, but you don't always want to waste the money on a late-night order. With only a few ingredients, this pizza quesadilla can be dressed up or down depending on what you're craving. Keep it simple with pepperoni and cheese, or get creative by adding a few tablespoons of leftover chopped vegetables, cooked crumbled sausage, or sliced olives. If you like spicy, try adding sliced pickled jalapeños straight from the jar. Plus, adding pizza sauce for dipping is a can't miss tip! If you're really short on time, assemble the quesadilla on a microwave-safe plate, microwave for 45 seconds, and enjoy.

Ingredients

1 (10") flour tortilla

1/2 cup shredded mozzarella cheese

7 slices pepperoni

1 Warm a nonstick skillet over medium heat. Place tortilla into the skillet and sprinkle cheese onto half of tortilla. Top cheese with pepperoni and fold tortilla in half, covering cheese and pepperoni.

2 Cook tortilla for 3 minutes or until golden brown and crispy, then flip and cook the other side for an additional 3 minutes. When done, both sides will be browned, and cheese will be melted. Serve warm.

Per Serving: Calories: 409; Fat: 16g; Sodium: 1,049mg; Carbohydrates: 40g; Fiber: 2g; Sugar: 3g; Protein: 19g

Pan-Seared Strip Steak

Prep Time: 5 minutes **Cook Time:** 10 minutes **Serves 1**

When you want to treat yourself to something fancy but cost-effective, look no further than strip steak. It's a lean cut of meat that's often much more budget-friendly than rib eye or filet mignon. When cooked properly, this tender cut of meat goes well with your choice of sides, from baked potatoes to pasta or even a side of blackened shrimp for a surf and turf dinner. This recipe uses coconut oil for searing due to its high smoke point, but if you're a fan of buttery flavor, top your finished steak with a small pat of butter after it's done cooking.

Ingredients

1 (8-ounce) New York strip steak

1 teaspoon McCormick Montreal Steak Seasoning

2 tablespoons refined coconut oil

1 Warm a skillet over medium-high heat. Sprinkle all sides of steak with seasoning.

2 Melt coconut oil in the skillet. Place steak into the skillet and let it cook for 3 minutes without moving it. Turn and repeat on the opposite side. Pick up steak with tongs and quickly sear the edges of steak, about 45 seconds each. When done, steak should have an internal temperature of at least 140°F for a medium-cooked finish and have a browned crust.

3 Let steak rest for 10 minutes, then slice to serve.

Per Serving: Calories: 565; Fat: 34g; Sodium: 795mg; Carbohydrates: 0g; Fiber: 0g; Sugar: 0g; Protein: 55g

Garlic Butter Steak Bites

Prep Time: 5 minutes **Cook Time:** 6 minutes **Serves 1**

Steak bites are a great way to treat yourself and flex your culinary skills. Steak doesn't need a lot of seasoning to taste great, just a good sear on the stove with some salt to let its natural flavor shine. For this recipe, you can use pre-minced garlic from a jar or freshly mince your own. Be sure to use real, quality butter such as Kerrygold for the best taste, not a stick of margarine or a butter spread. Sirloin is a budget-friendly option, but feel free to use any cut of lean steak you have on hand.

Ingredients

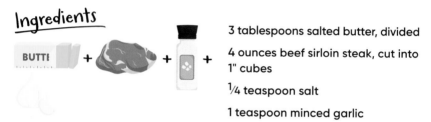

3 tablespoons salted butter, divided

4 ounces beef sirloin steak, cut into 1" cubes

¼ teaspoon salt

1 teaspoon minced garlic

1 Warm a skillet over medium-high heat. Add 2 tablespoons of butter to the skillet. Sprinkle steak with salt on all sides, and then add steak to the skillet. Sear steak on each side for about 45 seconds or until browned.

2 Add remaining tablespoon of butter and garlic to the skillet and turn off the heat. For 2 minutes, occasionally spoon pan drippings on top of steak. When done, steak bites should have an internal temperature of 140°F for a medium-cooked finish. Place steak on a serving plate, let stand for 5 minutes, and then serve.

Per Serving: Calories: 549; Fat: 45g; Sodium: 904mg; Carbohydrates: 1g; Fiber: 0g; Sugar: 0g; Protein: 26g

Easy Skillet Burgers

Prep Time: 5 minutes **Cook Time:** 8 minutes **Serves 2**

Making burgers at home is easy, thanks to seasoned salt (a blend of various spices and salt). This seasoning cuts down on time spent measuring and adds great flavor to all kinds of meat. You can make these delicious burgers into patty melts by tucking the cooked patties into a grilled cheese, or serve them on a fluffy restaurant-style bun. Enjoy your burger plain or loaded up with your favorite toppings. Try lettuce, pickles, tomatoes, and American cheese for a classic burger, or make it a barbecue burger with crunchy fried onion pieces, barbecue sauce, and melty pepper jack cheese.

Ingredients

½ pound 80/20 ground beef

¾ teaspoon Worcestershire sauce

½ teaspoon seasoned salt

1 Warm a nonstick skillet over medium heat. Place beef into a medium bowl and pour in Worcestershire sauce. Work the sauce into beef using your hands.

2 Separate beef into two balls. Form the balls into 5"-wide patties. Sprinkle seasoned salt onto both sides of each patty.

3 Place patties into the skillet and cook for 4 minutes per side. When finished, the internal temperature should be 160°F for well-done, and burgers should have a brown crust on the outside. Serve warm.

Per Serving: Calories: 192; Fat: 10g; Sodium: 464mg; Carbohydrates: 0g; Fiber: 0g; Sugar: 0g; Protein: 19g

Ham and Cheese Pinwheels

Prep Time: 10 minutes **Cook Time:** 15 minutes **Makes 12** (serving size: 3 pinwheels)

These pinwheels are filling enough to be a meal—plus, leftovers make an excellent snack. Filled with gooey cheese and smoky ham, these pinwheels are fun and easy. This recipe uses the entire can of pizza crust, meaning it's great to share with friends or save as leftovers. You can store leftovers in an airtight container in the refrigerator for up to 4 days and microwave for 1 minute to reheat. For an eye-catching presentation, brush the tops before baking with a little melted butter, sprinkle with Everything but the Bagel seasoning, and serve with guacamole.

Ingredients

1 tube Pillsbury refrigerated Classic Pizza Crust

1 cup shredded mild Cheddar cheese

8 ounces thinly sliced deli Black Forest ham

1 Preheat the oven to 425°F. Line a baking sheet with parchment paper and set aside.

2 On a clean work surface, unroll pizza dough. Gently press it out to about ¼" thickness. Sprinkle evenly with cheese and press cheese gently into dough. Top with ham slices.

3 Starting at one of the short ends of the dough, tightly roll into a log. Firmly press the seam together to prevent it from coming apart.

4 Slice dough into twelve (1"-wide) pieces. Place pinwheels on the prepared baking sheet and bake for 15 minutes or until golden brown and the cheese is melted. Serve warm.

Per Serving: Calories: 415; Fat: 14g; Sodium: 1,370mg; Carbohydrates: 50g; Fiber: 1g; Sugar: 7g; Protein: 23g

Chili Cheese Fries

Prep Time: 5 minutes **Cook Time:** 20 minutes **Serves 2**

These loaded fries are perfect for late nights or game-day eats. Seasoned fries add a ton of flavor and make an excellent base for this cheesy comfort food. Feel free to use your favorite brand of beef chili, or opt for vegetarian chili. If you want to load these fries up, sour cream, chopped red onions, and sliced pickled jalapeños are easy options that don't take time to prepare. For those days when you want only chili cheese dip, you can omit the fries and enjoy with tortilla chips or Fritos scoops as dippers.

Ingredients

6 ounces frozen Checkers/Rally's Famous Seasoned Fries

1 cup Hormel No Beans Chili

¼ cup Kraft Cheez Whiz Original Cheese Dip

1 Preheat the oven to 425°F. Line a baking sheet with aluminum foil, and then place fries on top. Bake for 20 minutes or until golden brown and crispy.

2 While fries are cooking, place chili into a medium microwave-safe bowl. Cover the bowl with a small microwave-safe plate. Microwave for 3 minutes, stirring halfway through cooking time. When done, stir Cheez Whiz into the chili until well combined.

3 Spoon chili and cheese mixture on top of fries, coating as many as possible. Serve warm.

Per Serving: Calories: 382; Fat: 18g; Sodium: 1,430mg; Carbohydrates: 34g; Fiber: 4g; Sugar: 5g; Protein: 13g

Barbecue Meatballs

Prep Time: 5 minutes **Cook Time:** 20 minutes **Serves 2**

Perfect for pairing alongside Kraft Easy Mac or Jiffy corn bread, these sweet and smoky meatballs require very little effort. Simmering them in barbecue sauce helps them absorb the flavor, and you can choose your favorite sauce to customize them. Additionally, while this recipe was created for the saucepan, if you happen to have a slow cooker on hand, you can also scale the recipe to feed all your roommates; let the meatballs slow cook on low for 6 hours for a hot and easy meal.

Ingredients

8 frozen Johnsonville Homestyle Meatballs

¼ cup Sweet Baby Ray's Original Barbecue Sauce

¼ cup water

Combine all ingredients in a medium saucepan over medium heat. Bring to a boil, then reduce to a simmer for 18 minutes. Meatballs should be heated through and sauce should be thick enough to coat meatballs. Serve warm.

Per Serving: Calories: 456; Fat: 35g; Sodium: 1,063mg; Carbohydrates: 25g; Fiber: 0g; Sugar: 18g; Protein: 12g

Salsa Verde Pulled Pork Tacos

Prep Time: 5 minutes **Cook Time:** 2 minutes **Makes 4** (serving size: 2 tacos)

Salsa verde is made from tomatillos, giving it a vibrant green color. Garlic and spices give it flavor that's a great alternative to red salsa. This salsa in combination with pulled pork is delicious. In this recipe, you'll use pre-cooked plain pulled pork to make your tacos. Some grocery stores prepare their pork fresh daily, so it can be easy to find near the freshly made hot-food section in the deli. Try topping your tacos with sour cream, crumbled cotija cheese, lettuce, beans, or pico de gallo.

Ingredients

6 ounces cooked pulled pork

¼ cup Old El Paso Creamy Salsa Verde Sauce

4 (6") yellow corn tortillas

1 Place pork into a medium microwave-safe bowl. Microwave for 1 minute 30 seconds or until heated through. Remove from the microwave, add salsa on top of pork, and stir until well combined.

2 Wrap tortillas in a damp paper towel and put them on a small microwave-safe plate. Place into the microwave and cook for 30 seconds or until hot.

3 Divide pork mixture evenly among tortillas, fold in half, and serve warm.

Per Serving: Calories: 327; Fat: 12g; Sodium: 807mg; Carbohydrates: 39g; Fiber: 4g; Sugar: 13g; Protein: 14g

CHAPTER 8

VEGETARIAN MAIN DISHES

Whether you're cooking for your friends with food restrictions, incorporating a Meatless Monday into your weekly routine, or living life as a full-fledged vegetarian, this chapter will be an excellent guide for your success in the kitchen.

Loaded with fresh, nutrient-rich ingredients that are bursting with flavor, these recipes make satisfying main dishes that you'll keep coming back to (even if you eat meat regularly). The recipes in the pages ahead are filling, diverse, and straightforward, offering you a plethora of new ideas without an ounce of meat in sight.

This chapter shows that you don't have to only eat salads to enjoy a plant-based diet, but you can use meatless meals as a way to experience new types of food. You'll satisfy your taste buds and add surprising variety to your meal plan with delicious recipes like Creamy Feta Pasta and crunchy Black Bean Tostadas, while mastering a Microwave Baked Potato that cooks in just minutes. Plus, you'll also learn how to round out the flavors of the recipes and expand on the entrées to make them into full meat-free meals.

White Cheddar Pesto Pasta

Prep Time: 5 minutes **Cook Time:** 3 minutes 30 seconds **Serves 1**

Elevate your mac and cheese cups with the fresh and herbaceous flavor of pesto. The microwavable pasta is an excellent pantry staple for busy days, and with just a couple extra ingredients, this simple dish can be transformed into an upgraded entrée. Serve alongside a salad or a piece of crusty bread for a filling comfort meal.

Ingredients

¼ cup fresh baby spinach, loosely packed

1 (2.39-ounce) Kraft Deluxe White Cheddar Mac & Cheese Cup

1 tablespoon basil pesto

1 Place spinach on a cutting board and chop finely. Set aside.

2 Uncover macaroni cup and remove cheese sauce pouch. Fill cup with water to the fill line imprinted on the inside of the cup.

3 Microwave for 3 minutes 30 seconds or until pasta is tender.

4 Stir in cheese sauce, spinach, and pesto. Place a small plate on top of the cup and set aside for 2 minutes. Remove plate and stir until creamy. Serve warm.

Per Serving: Calories: 281; Fat: 14g; Sodium: 665mg; Carbohydrates: 32g; Fiber: 1g; Sugar: 5g; Protein: 8g

Creamy Feta Pasta

Prep Time: 5 minutes **Cook Time:** 6 minutes **Serves 1**

Feta cheese is an essential ingredient to have in your refrigerator. It's great for pasta because it eliminates the need to use heavy cream in order to get a velvety sauce; plus, leftover feta is perfect to use in your salads and dips. This wonderful cheese combined with the juiciness of the cherry tomatoes, and the no-water-needed Ready Pasta that already includes salt and olive oil, means you're in for a quick meal that's also an explosion of flavor.

Ingredients

1 (7-ounce) package Barilla Ready Pasta Penne

½ cup crumbled feta cheese

1 cup halved cherry tomatoes

1 Knead package to break apart pasta. Warm a nonstick skillet over medium heat and empty pasta into the skillet. Warm pasta for 4 minutes or until heated through.

2 Add feta and tomatoes to the skillet. Gently stir until feta is melted and tomatoes begin to soften, about 2 minutes. A light pink sauce will begin to coat noodles, and become creamy when done. Serve warm.

Per Serving: Calories: 538; Fat: 18g; Sodium: 1,057mg; Carbohydrates: 77g; Fiber: 10g; Sugar: 7g; Protein: 24g

Easy Smothered Burrito

Prep Time: 5 minutes **Cook Time:** 1 minute 30 seconds **Serves 1**

It's never been easier to upgrade your frozen burrito into a full-on entrée that tastes homemade. And while you're free to let your creativity run wild with flavoring this dish, only a couple of extra ingredients are needed to transform it. For a twist, use your favorite frozen burrito and add fresh toppings such as chopped lettuce and tomato.

Ingredients

1 frozen El Monterey Bean & Cheese Burrito

2 tablespoons red enchilada sauce

2 tablespoons sour cream

1 Follow package instructions to microwave burrito, then set it aside.

2 Pour enchilada sauce into a small microwave-safe bowl and microwave for 15 seconds or until heated through. Pour sauce on top of burrito to cover it as evenly as possible, and then top with sour cream. Serve warm.

Per Serving: Calories: 258; Fat: 8g; Sodium: 521mg; Carbohydrates: 36g; Fiber: 4g; Sugar: 3g; Protein: 8g

Black Bean Tostadas

Prep Time: 5 minutes **Cook Time:** 5 minutes **Serves 1**

Skip the drive-through and make a batch of fresh and flavorful tostadas right at home. Rich in protein and loaded with complementary Mexican-style flavors, this meal hits all the right savory notes and comes together in just minutes. Feel free to customize tostadas with your favorite toppings such as crumbled cotija cheese, sour cream, corn, or a dash of hot sauce.

Ingredients

½ cup canned black beans, drained and rinsed

¼ teaspoon salt

2 (6") Mission Estilo Casero Tostadas

¼ cup fresh Del Monte Pico de Gallo

1 Preheat the oven to 350°F. Line a baking sheet with parchment paper.

2 Using a fork, mash beans in a small bowl. Season with salt and mash again to fully combine.

3 Place tostadas on the prepared baking sheet. Top with mashed beans. Bake for 5 minutes or until tostadas are crispy. Top each tostada with 2 tablespoons pico de gallo and serve.

Per Serving: Calories: 279; Fat: 6g; Sodium: 1,822mg; Carbohydrates: 46g; Fiber: 10g; Sugar: 1g; Protein: 10g

Microwave Baked Potato

Prep Time: 5 minutes **Cook Time:** 8 minutes **Serves 1**

Potatoes are vitamin C–rich root vegetables with an endless number of ways to customize their flavor. They're also inexpensive and ready to eat in no time. Because of this, it's important to know how to properly cook a "baked" potato in your microwave, for those times when you need a hearty and filling reminder of home. Plus, you can easily load up the potato with all your favorite fixings such as sour cream, Cheddar cheese, chives, and more.

Ingredients

1 medium russet potato

¼ teaspoon salt

1 tablespoon salted butter

1 Use a fork to pierce potato about ten times all over, to allow steam to escape.

2 Place potato on a microwave-safe plate. Microwave for 8 minutes, turning potato over halfway through cooking time. When done, a fork should easily go through potato.

3 Let stand for 2 minutes, then cut potato in half lengthwise. Sprinkle the inside with salt, top with butter, and serve.

Per Serving: Calories: 261; Fat: 11g; Sodium: 689mg; Carbohydrates: 37g; Fiber: 4g; Sugar: 2g; Protein: 4g

Cacio e Pepe

Prep Time: 5 minutes **Cook Time:** 12 minutes **Serves 2**

Cacio e Pepe (Italian for "cheese and pepper") is a deceivingly simple dish that will add elegance to your mealtime with both the name and the presentation. This meal for two is easy to put together on the stovetop and can be served with a light salad, roasted vegetables, or even turkey meatballs if you feel like you might need to add a little something extra.

Ingredients

3 cups water

1/2 teaspoon salt

4 ounces dry pot-size spaghetti

1 tablespoon salted butter

1/3 cup grated Parmesan cheese

1/4 teaspoon ground black pepper

1 In a medium saucepan over high heat, bring water and salt to a boil.

2 Add spaghetti to the saucepan, reduce heat to medium, and cook for 8 minutes or until al dente. Then, use a measuring cup to carefully scoop out 1/4 cup of pasta water and set it aside. Drain remaining pasta water using a colander.

3 Turn off the heat and return the saucepan to the stovetop. Add butter and stir spaghetti until coated in butter. Pour reserved pasta water back into the saucepan along with Parmesan and stir until a creamy, light sauce forms, about 2 minutes. When done, sauce will coat spaghetti, but not be excessively liquidly in the pan. Sprinkle pepper on top of spaghetti and serve. Store leftovers in an airtight container in the refrigerator for up to 3 days for the best taste.

Per Serving: Calories: 340; Fat: 10g; Sodium: 529mg; Carbohydrates: 45g; Fiber: 3g; Sugar: 1g; Protein: 13g

Cheesy Ravioli Lasagna

Prep Time: 5 minutes **Cook Time:** 20 minutes **Serves 2**

This pasta-swapping shortcut will give you all the taste of the classic dish with a lot less effort. Frozen ravioli is filled with soft cheeses, similar to those you find in lasagna. With this recipe, you won't need to boil noodles or mix up a long list of ingredients. Even better, it's budget-friendly and only takes 5 minutes of prep time. Grab your favorite salad kit and a loaf of garlic bread at the store for a full Italian-inspired meal that's as convenient as it is delicious.

Ingredients

1½ cups marinara sauce, divided

16 frozen Louisa Four Cheese Ravioli

1 cup shredded mozzarella cheese, divided

1 Preheat the oven to 400°F.

2 Spread ½ cup sauce onto the bottom of a 1-quart baking dish. Arrange 8 ravioli in a single layer over sauce and sprinkle with ½ cup cheese.

3 Top with ½ cup sauce. Place remaining 8 ravioli in a single layer over sauce. Pour remaining ½ cup sauce over the top and sprinkle with remaining ½ cup cheese.

4 Bake for 20 minutes or until bubbly and lightly browned. Allow 10 minutes to cool, then serve.

Per Serving: Calories: 443; Fat: 17g; Sodium: 1,450mg; Carbohydrates: 46g; Fiber: 5g; Sugar: 13g; Protein: 23g

Creamy Fettuccine Alfredo with Broccoli

Prep Time: 5 minutes **Cook Time:** 25 minutes **Serves 2**

This creamy pasta dish can be found right at the intersection of easy and cheesy. Plus, the addition of broccoli adds a complementary flavor profile to satisfy your taste buds and adds a boost of healthy nutrients to keep you feeling good. If you love spice, be sure to sprinkle on some crushed red pepper flakes to kick this recipe up a notch. This recipe uses fettuccine, but feel free to use penne, spaghetti, or any pasta you have on hand.

Ingredients

1 (10.8-ounce) bag frozen Birds Eye Steamfresh Broccoli Florets

1¼ cups water

4 ounces dry fettuccine

1¼ cups Bertolli Alfredo Sauce

1 Follow package instructions for microwaving broccoli, and set it aside.

2 Pour water into a medium saucepan and bring to a boil. Add pasta and Alfredo sauce, stirring gently. Reduce the heat to a simmer and cook for 10 minutes or until pasta is soft enough to stir.

3 Add cooked broccoli to the saucepan, cover with a lid, and cook for 5 minutes. When done, pasta should be softened and coated with creamy sauce. Serve warm.

Per Serving: Calories: 535; Fat: 29g; Sodium: 1,012mg; Carbohydrates: 56g; Fiber: 7g; Sugar: 3g; Protein: 17g

Lentil Taco Filling

Prep Time: 5 minutes **Cook Time:** 22 minutes **Serves 2**

If you're looking for a meat-free meal that won't break the bank, this taco filling is your go-to. Lentils are a powerhouse legume loaded with protein and fiber. They're easily stored in the pantry and are a great and filling choice for just about anyone! This recipe is perfect for tacos, burritos, and fajita bowls. There are brown, green, and red lentils, but for this recipe, brown lentils are ideal—they taste most similar to refried beans!

Ingredients

½ cup dry brown lentils

1½ cups water

½ cup mild salsa

3 tablespoons taco seasoning

1 Rinse lentils in a fine-mesh strainer. Remove any damaged lentils or debris.

2 Combine all ingredients in a medium saucepan over high heat. Bring to a boil, then cover and reduce the heat to simmer for 20 minutes. When done, lentils should be tender and have a deep brown color. Serve warm.

Per Serving: Calories: 171; Fat: 0g; Sodium: 1,385mg; Carbohydrates: 31g; Fiber: 12g; Sugar: 7g; Protein: 10g

Vegetable Potpie with Biscuit Crust

Prep Time: 5 minutes **Cook Time:** 22 minutes **Serves 8**

This recipe proves that you don't need chicken to get all of the enjoyable flavors out of a hearty potpie. Doubling down on the vegetables without missing a beat, this delicious meal is the perfect and comforting quick dinner to whip up during the colder months. Subbing for pie crust, the biscuit crust makes it even more simple. No cutting or rolling is required, and you still get to enjoy a buttery, flaky crust. This recipe makes a large batch, making it perfect for a dinner with friends or meal prep for the week. Store covered in the refrigerator for up to 4 days.

Ingredients

1 (10.5-ounce) can Campbell's Cream of Celery Soup

1 (15-ounce) can Veg-All Original Mixed Vegetables, drained

1 (16.3-ounce) can Pillsbury Grands Southern Homestyle Buttermilk Biscuits

1 Preheat the oven to 400°F and spray a 9" × 9" baking dish with nonstick cooking spray.

2 In a medium bowl, stir together soup and vegetables. Pour into the prepared dish and spread into an even layer.

3 Arrange biscuits on top of soup mixture in two rows of four, leaving an inch between them. Bake for 22 minutes or until soup mixture is bubbling and the biscuits are fluffy and browned. Let cool for 10 minutes, then scoop onto plates to serve.

Per Serving: Calories: 225; Fat: 9g; Sodium: 738mg; Carbohydrates: 33g; Fiber: 2g; Sugar: 1g; Protein: 4g

Chickpea Tikka Masala

Prep Time: 5 minutes **Cook Time:** 20 minutes **Serves 2**

This tomato-based dish is filled with warming spices for a cozy and tasty meal. Canned chickpeas make this recipe easier than ever and add a nutty, earthy quality to each bite. Serve alongside warm naan, often found in the deli section of the grocery store. Try with a tablespoon of chopped cilantro and a drizzle of plain Greek yogurt for a bright and zingy flavor.

Ingredients

1 (15-ounce) can chickpeas, drained

1 cup Patak's Tikka Masala Curry Simmer Sauce

1 (8.5-ounce) pouch Ben's Original Basmati Ready Rice

1 Warm a medium saucepan over medium heat. Add chickpeas and curry sauce, and stir to combine. Bring to a gentle boil, then reduce heat and simmer for 18 minutes.

2 Follow package instructions for microwaving rice, then set aside.

3 When chickpeas are done, they will be soft and coated in sauce. To serve, separate rice into two portions and place portions of chickpea mixture (including sauce) on top. Serve warm.

Per Serving: Calories: 455; Fat: 9g; Sodium: 629mg; Carbohydrates: 79g; Fiber: 9g; Sugar: 9g; Protein: 14g

Vegetable Stir-Fry

Prep Time: 5 minutes **Cook Time:** 10 minutes **Serves 2**

This recipe is a great way to enjoy a tasty and nutritious blend of vegetables without any hassle. The stir-fry sauce adds a flavorful zing that brings the ingredients together, creating a crave-worthy meal to add to your weekly rotation. If you're following a vegetarian or vegan lifestyle, be sure to check the nutritional labels of your sauce closely for ingredients like oyster sauce and beef broth, which are commonly used by different brands.

Ingredients

1 (10.8-ounce) bag frozen Birds Eye Steamfresh Broccoli, Carrots, Sugar Snap Peas, & Water Chestnuts

1/3 cup House of Tsang Szechuan Spicy Stir-Fry Sauce

1 (8.5-ounce) pouch Ben's Original Jasmine Ready Rice

1 Follow package instructions to microwave frozen vegetables.

2 Warm a skillet over medium heat, and add cooked vegetables into the skillet. Pour stir-fry sauce on top of vegetables. Sauté for 2 minutes, stirring occasionally, until all vegetables are coated with sauce and are tender.

3 Follow package instructions for microwaving rice.

4 Divide rice between two bowls and top with equal amounts of stir-fry vegetables, including any leftover pan sauce. Serve warm.

Per Serving: Calories: 347; Fat: 3g; Sodium: 1,530mg; Carbohydrates: 70g; Fiber: 5g; Sugar: 13g; Protein: 8g

CHAPTER 9

DESSERTS

Arguably just as fulfilling of a food as any meal, desserts are a powerful force that binds all that have a sweet tooth. From decadent chocolate indulgences to light and tasty fruit-based treats, these dishes comfort us after a long day, help us celebrate accomplishments among friends, and kick our cravings to the curb.

Desserts are a delicious and exciting part of the culinary scene, so it's crucial that you're equipped with only the best dessert recipes to take with you throughout your college experience. This group of recipes tastes great, can be thrown together at a moment's notice, and will satisfy those cravings that happen any time of day. Plus, if you're someone who's intimidated by baking, that's totally fine. This chapter breaks down all of its recipes into very manageable ingredient lists with simple steps. These recipes allow you to whip up something special that always hits the spot, whether you're celebrating your roommate's birthday, burning the midnight oil, or winding down after dinner on a random Tuesday.

From tart and tasty Raspberry Lime Sorbet to sugary sweet Birthday Cake Mix Cookies, you can consider your cravings conquered, no matter the occasion!

Raspberry Lime Sorbet

Prep Time: 5 minutes **Cook Time:** N/A **Serves 1**

Frozen fruit is an affordable option that comes in bags small enough to throw in your dorm's freezer. Then, when the mood for a bright and fruity treat strikes, you'll be ready to tackle it in minutes. While the recipe was designed with raspberries, you can easily swap them out for strawberries or mixed berries depending on your flavor preference.

Ingredients

1 1/2 cups frozen raspberries

Juice and zest of 1/2 small lime

1/2 tablespoon honey

1 Place raspberries into a small bowl and allow them to sit at room temperature for 5 minutes. This allows them to slightly defrost and make a smoother sorbet.

2 Transfer raspberries to a blender with lime juice, zest, and honey. Blend on high for 45 seconds or until smooth. Scoop sorbet into a small bowl and serve immediately.

Per Serving: Calories: 143; Fat: 0g; Sodium: 2mg; Carbohydrates: 35g; Fiber: 14g; Sugar: 18g; Protein: 3g

Strawberry Frozen Yogurt

Prep Time: 5 minutes **Cook Time:** N/A **Serves 1**

Satisfying your Froyo cravings has never been easier. So, pull out your blender and get ready to mix up a dose of creamy frozen bliss. Top it with a helping of whipped cream to double down on texture, while also stepping up the presentation. If you prefer a sweeter treat, you can use vanilla Greek yogurt, drizzle 1 teaspoon of honey on top of your blended yogurt, or use a squirt of your preferred liquid sweetener.

Ingredients

¾ cup low-fat plain Greek yogurt

1 cup frozen strawberry slices

Place yogurt and strawberry slices into the blender. Blend on high for 1 minute or until mostly smooth. When done, yogurt should be light pink and have some small chunks of strawberries remaining. It will be thick and creamy like soft-serve ice cream. Serve cold.

Per Serving: Calories: 179; Fat: 3g; Sodium: 58mg; Carbohydrates: 20g; Fiber: 3g; Sugar: 14g; Protein: 18g

No-Bake Cheesecake Fluff

Prep Time: 20 minutes **Cook Time:** N/A **Serves 2**

Traditional cheesecakes are delicious, but they take a long time to make, and they often have a list of ingredients that will exhaust you just by reading it. This simplified cheesecake gives you all of the same flavor in a fluffy, no-bake bowl that you can share with a friend. To re-create that classic cheesecake crust, you can sprinkle on crushed graham crackers. Make the recipe your own by adding chopped fresh fruit or a drizzle of caramel sauce for an indulgent treat. Use a hand mixer for this recipe instead of the plastic spatula if you have one.

Ingredients

4 ounces cream cheese, softened

2 tablespoons granulated sugar

2 cups Cool Whip Original Whipped Topping

1 In a large bowl, use a plastic spatula to beat cream cheese and sugar together until completely smooth and fluffy. Use a rubber spatula to gently stir Cool Whip into cream cheese mixture. When done, mixture should be very light and fluffy.

2 Cover the bowl with plastic wrap and place into the refrigerator to chill for at least 15 minutes. Serve.

Per Serving: Calories: 441; Fat: 29g; Sodium: 206mg; Carbohydrates: 39g; Fiber: 0g; Sugar: 30g; Protein: 3g

Peanut Butter Cups

Prep Time: 10 minutes **Cook Time:** 1 minute **Makes 8** (serving size: 1 P.B. cup)

Forget your store-bought favorites! With just a few simple ingredients, you can throw together this high-quality, speedy, and delicious treat. Use almond or cashew butter or even Wowbutter or SunButter as an alternative to peanut butter.

Ingredients

⅔ cup creamy peanut butter

¼ cup confectioners' sugar

2 cups milk chocolate chips

1 Place eight silicone cupcake molds on a large plate and set aside.

2 In a small bowl, mix peanut butter and sugar until well combined and creamy.

3 Place chocolate chips into a medium microwave-safe bowl and microwave for 30 seconds. Stir chocolate chips and microwave for additional 15-second intervals, stirring in-between, until chocolate is melted and smooth.

4 Place 1 tablespoon of melted chocolate into the bottom of each cupcake mold. Carefully move the plate with the cupcake molds to the refrigerator for 10 minutes so that chocolate can firm up. Next, place about 1 tablespoon of peanut butter mixture on top of each chocolate layer, spreading as evenly as possible.

5 Pour 1 tablespoon of melted chocolate on top of peanut butter and smooth it into an even layer. Place the plate with peanut butter cups into the refrigerator for at least 1 hour or until firm, then serve. Alternatively, you can freeze them for 15 minutes. Store leftovers in an airtight container in the refrigerator for up to 4 days.

Per Serving: Calories: 365; Fat: 22g; Sodium: 36mg; Carbohydrates: 33g; Fiber: 3g; Sugar: 27g; Protein: 8g

Oreo Ice Cream Pie

Prep Time: 15 minutes **Cook Time:** N/A **Serves 8**

If you're a fan of all things cookies and cream, this easy frozen pie is the perfect treat to whip up for your next movie night. Wonderfully creamy, with the satisfying crunch of Oreos in every bite, this recipe is sure to impress. Plus, it leaves no hints of just how simple it was to put together. Customize this recipe by using your favorite flavor of ice cream or swapping the Oreos for another cookie like Chips Ahoy.

Ingredients

1 quart vanilla bean ice cream, softened

20 Oreo cookies, divided

1 (6-ounce) chocolate cookie pie crust

1 Scoop ice cream into an extra-large mixing bowl. Place 10 Oreos into a sealable storage bag and use a rolling pin to crush into bite-sized pieces. Gently stir Oreo pieces into ice cream.

2 Scrape ice cream and cookie mixture into pie crust and smooth into an even layer. Using the same storage bag from step one, crush remaining Oreos with the rolling pin into crumbs. Then, sprinkle powder all over the top of pie in an even layer. Cover pie with plastic wrap and place into the freezer for 4 hours to set. Let come to room temperature for 10 minutes before serving. Store leftovers covered in the freezer for up to 2 weeks.

Per Serving: Calories: 367; Fat: 17g; Sodium: 260mg; Carbohydrates: 50g; Fiber: 1g; Sugar: 33g; Protein: 5g

Birthday Cake Mix Cookies

Prep Time: 5 minutes **Cook Time:** 15 minutes **Makes 12** (serving size: 1 cookie)

Got a birthday to celebrate? For a creative alternative to a classic birthday cake, surprise your friends with a batch of Funfetti-flavored, freshly baked cookies. You can even take this dessert to the next level by grabbing a tub of Funfetti frosting to make yummy cookie sandwiches. One of the best parts about this recipe is that any flavor cake mix can be substituted. So, if you're a fan of chocolate, red velvet, or even lemon cake, you can customize these easy cake mix cookies.

Ingredients

1 (15.25-ounce) box Pillsbury Funfetti Premium Cake and Cupcake Mix

⅓ cup vegetable oil

2 large eggs

1 Preheat the oven to 350°F. Line a baking sheet with parchment paper and set aside.

2 In a large bowl, mix together cake mix, oil, and eggs until well combined.

3 Scoop 2 tablespoons of dough and roll into a ball, then place on the prepared baking sheet. Repeat with remaining dough.

4 Bake cookies for 15 minutes or until the edges are lightly browned and the centers no longer appear wet. Cool for 10 minutes, then serve. Store leftovers in an airtight container for up to 3 days.

Per Serving: Calories: 200; Fat: 8g; Sodium: 296mg; Carbohydrates: 29g; Fiber: 1g; Sugar: 15g; Protein: 2g

Chocolate Mousse

Prep Time: 5 minutes **Cook Time:** N/A **Serves 1**

Chocolate mousse has a reputation for elegance, but it really is a shockingly simple recipe that takes no time to make. This recipe simplifies the process even further for a light and airy treat designed to be prepared at any time. Feel free to use dark chocolate pudding or even white chocolate pudding to switch things up. You can enjoy it right out of the bowl, or you can scoop it into a dessert glass and layer with additional whipped cream and berries for a special occasion.

Ingredients

1 (3.25-ounce) milk chocolate pudding cup

¾ cup Cool Whip Original Whipped Topping

Scoop pudding into a medium bowl. Gently stir in Cool Whip until no white streaks remain and pudding is a light, airy consistency. Enjoy immediately, or cover and put in the refrigerator for 1 hour if you want a firmer texture.

Per Serving: Calories: 280; Fat: 13g; Sodium: 140mg; Carbohydrates: 39g; Fiber: 0g; Sugar: 28g; Protein: 2g

Dark Chocolate Almond Nut Clusters

Prep Time: 10 minutes **Cook Time:** 1 minute **Makes 16** (serving size: 2 nut clusters)

These nut clusters are basically a simple way to make your own candy. All you need is your microwave to put together this treat. This recipe makes a big batch to enjoy all week, or you can share with friends. Feel free to customize these clusters with your favorite chocolate, add drizzles of white chocolate, or use a different nut. Just be sure to use the roasted almonds found in the snack aisle, rather than the plain raw almonds from the baking aisle. Roasted almonds are softer and will taste better because they have been baked.

Ingredients

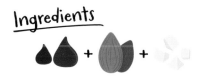

1 cup dark chocolate chips

1 cup roasted whole almonds

2 teaspoons flaky sea salt

1 Line a baking sheet with parchment paper and set aside.

2 Place chocolate chips into a medium microwave-safe bowl and microwave for 45 seconds. Stir chocolate chips and microwave them for another 15 seconds, then stir until fully melted and smooth.

3 Place almonds into chocolate and stir to fully coat. Use a spoon to drop small mounds of chocolate and almonds onto the prepared baking sheet, about 2 tablespoons per cluster. Leave 2" of space between clusters to avoid melting together. There should be sixteen clusters. Sprinkle each with 1/8 teaspoon sea salt.

4 Place clusters on the baking sheet into the refrigerator for 1 hour to harden. Store leftovers in an airtight container for up to 5 days.

Per Serving: Calories: 263; Fat: 19g; Sodium: 390mg; Carbohydrates: 20g; Fiber: 4g; Sugar: 13g; Protein: 4g

Cookie Butter Apple "Nachos"

Prep Time: 5 minutes **Cook Time:** 30 seconds **Serves 1**

Caramel and apples are a classic duo, but cookie butter is the upgrade you've been needing. Rich, creamy, and sweet, the spiced cookie butter used in this recipe is made from crushed speculoos caramel-flavored cookies; it makes the perfect topping for tart green apples. Dress up your "nachos" as much or as little as you'd like. Crumbles of Heath bars and a spoonful of whipped cream will make this apple-based dish feel truly indulgent. If cookie butter isn't your thing, you can use nut butter or even Nutella to enjoy this fun treat.

Ingredients

2 tablespoons Lotus Biscoff Cookie Butter

1 large Granny Smith apple, sliced into ¼"-thick slices

2 tablespoons milk chocolate chips

1 Place cookie butter into a small microwave-safe bowl and microwave for 30 seconds. Stir.

2 Arrange apple slices in a single layer on a plate. Drizzle warmed cookie butter over apple slices. Sprinkle with chocolate chips and serve.

Per Serving: Calories: 306; Fat: 9g Sodium: 75mg; Carbohydrates: 52g; Fiber: 6g; Sugar: 37g; Protein: 4g

M&M's Fudge

Prep Time: 5 minutes **Cook Time:** 3 minutes **Serves 12**

Fudge is such a great dessert because it's very easy to make, excellent for sharing, and highly customizable. This version uses M&M's to step up its fun and flavor, but you can take this recipe anywhere you choose; try adding chopped nuts, white chocolate chips, or even crushed Oreos. The toughest part about making this recipe is waiting for it to set, but if you can't help yourself, a little nibble won't hurt! If you don't have an 8" × 8" pan, feel free to scoop the dough evenly into twelve lined muffin cups.

Ingredients

1 (14-ounce) can sweetened condensed milk

1 cup milk chocolate chips

1/2 cup milk chocolate M&M's

1 Pour condensed milk into a large microwave-safe bowl. Microwave for 3 minutes, then stir in chocolate chips until completely smooth and well combined.

2 Line an 8" × 8" baking pan with parchment paper. Scrape chocolate mixture into the pan and scatter M&M's across the top evenly. Place in the refrigerator for 4 hours to set, then slice and serve. Store leftovers in an airtight container for up to 5 days.

Per Serving: Calories: 223; Fat: 8g; Sodium: 58mg; Carbohydrates: 32g; Fiber: 1g; Sugar: 31g; Protein: 4g

Peanut Butter Cookies

Prep Time: 5 minutes **Cook Time:** 8 minutes **Makes 4** (serving size: 1 cookie)

It's hard to beat the simplicity and nostalgia of peanut butter cookies! Loaded with that familiar sweetness and nutty flavor in every bite, this small batch comes together quickly to have you indulging in no time. To get creative with this recipe, you can add ¼ cup of chocolate chips for a burst of decadence, or experiment with chunky peanut butter for a change in texture.

Ingredients

½ cup no-sugar-added creamy peanut butter

½ cup packed light brown sugar, plus 1 tablespoon, divided

1 large egg yolk

1 Preheat the oven to 350°F. Line a baking sheet with parchment paper and set aside.

2 In a medium bowl, mix peanut butter, ½ cup brown sugar, and egg yolk until well combined. Separate dough into four even balls.

3 Sprinkle a little of remaining brown sugar on top of each cookie and use a fork to press a crisscross pattern into the top, pressing dough down into a thick disc, about ½" thick. Bake cookies for 8 minutes or until browned at the edges. Let cool for 10 minutes and serve.

Per Serving: Calories: 311; Fat: 16g; Sodium: 65mg; Carbohydrates: 38g; Fiber: 3g; Sugar: 32g; Protein: 9g

Caramel-Stuffed Chocolate Chip Cookies

Prep Time: 10 minutes **Cook Time:** 13 minutes **Makes 12** (serving size: 1 cookie)

Add a sweet and gooey gourmet twist to your cookie dough with this simple recipe. Caramel is an excellent way to add even more indulgence to your cookies, and this method couldn't be easier. Just be sure to use the soft square caramels, because hard candy won't give you the chewy texture you want out of these cookies. This recipe utilizes the entire batch of cookies, which is perfect for holiday cookie parties and sharing, but feel free to whip up only a few at a time.

Ingredients

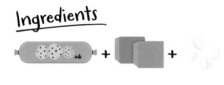

1 (16-ounce) package Nestlé Toll House Chocolate Chip Lovers Cookie Dough

12 Kraft Caramels, unwrapped

1½ teaspoons flaky sea salt

1 Preheat the oven to 350°F. Line a baking sheet with parchment paper and set aside.

2 Break apart cookie dough along the pre-cut lines to make twelve cookies. Roll a piece of dough into a disk and press a caramel into the center. Gently press dough around caramel so that caramel is fully enveloped in the center. Shape into a ball and place on the prepared baking sheet. Repeat with remaining cookie dough and caramels. Make sure cookies are at least 2" apart. (You may need to bake in batches.)

3 Bake for 13 minutes or until cookies are golden brown. Sprinkle the top of each cookie with ⅛ teaspoon sea salt. Cool for 10 minutes before serving. Store leftovers in an airtight container for up to 5 days.

Per Serving: Calories: 201; Fat: 9g; Sodium: 403mg; Carbohydrates: 29g; Fiber: 0g; Sugar: 19g; Protein: 2g

Blueberry Cinnamon Roll Bake

Prep Time: 10 minutes **Cook Time:** 20 minutes **Serves 4**

Cinnamon rolls aren't just for breakfast. They also serve as a convenient base for a delightfully indulgent dessert, like these enriched and delicious rolls. Fresh blueberries lighten up the decadent layers of rich and fluffy rolls, offering just the right amount of balance and scrumptious tang. If blueberries aren't your thing, feel free to swap them with juicy blackberries or sweet raspberries. Store leftovers covered in the refrigerator for up to 3 days.

Ingredients

1 (12.4-ounce) can Pillsbury Cinnamon Rolls with Cream Cheese Icing

1/2 cup sweetened condensed milk

1 cup fresh blueberries

1 Preheat the oven to 350°F. Spray an 8" round baking pan with nonstick cooking spray and set aside.

2 Open can of cinnamon rolls and set frosting packet aside. Cut each cinnamon roll into four equal pieces and place into the prepared pan, overlapping as needed. Pour condensed milk on top of cinnamon roll pieces and gently stir to coat.

3 Add blueberries to the pan, scattering evenly across cinnamon roll pieces.

4 Place the pan into the oven and bake for 20 minutes or until cinnamon rolls are puffy and browned. Let cool for 10 minutes, then drizzle frosting packet evenly across the top of baked dish. Serve warm.

Per Serving: Calories: 433; Fat: 6g; Sodium: 734mg; Carbohydrates: 73g; Fiber: 2g; Sugar: 43g; Protein: 7g

Mason Jar Vanilla Ice Cream

Prep Time: 5 minutes **Cook Time:** N/A **Serves 2**

This recipe makes for a tasty dessert, and it's also a fun and creative activity to do with your friends. One of the best parts is that you can customize any flavor you want with additions like fresh strawberries, chocolate chips, caramel sauce, or a few teaspoons of nuts or small candies. Be sure to use a 16-ounce Mason jar to allow the ingredients enough space to move around.

Ingredients

1 cup heavy whipping cream

1/3 cup sweetened condensed milk

1 teaspoon vanilla extract

1 Pour all ingredients into a 16-ounce Mason jar. Screw the lid on the jar and begin shaking vigorously for 5 minutes or until whipped cream forms in the jar. It will sound less sloshy and appear fluffy when done.

2 Place the jar into the freezer for 4 hours or until frozen, or remove after 3 hours for soft serve. Allow to soften 10 minutes at room temperature before serving. Store in the freezer for up to 2 months for the best taste.

Per Serving: Calories: 580; Fat: 46g; Sodium: 109mg; Carbohydrates: 31g; Fiber: 0g; Sugar: 31g; Protein: 6g

US/METRIC CONVERSION CHARTS

VOLUME CONVERSIONS

US Volume Measure	Metric Equivalent
1/8 teaspoon	0.5 milliliter
1/4 teaspoon	1 milliliter
1/2 teaspoon	2 milliliters
1 teaspoon	5 milliliters
1/2 tablespoon	7 milliliters
1 tablespoon (3 teaspoons)	15 milliliters
2 tablespoons (1 fluid ounce)	30 milliliters
1/4 cup (4 tablespoons)	60 milliliters
1/3 cup	90 milliliters
1/2 cup (4 fluid ounces)	125 milliliters
2/3 cup	160 milliliters
3/4 cup (6 fluid ounces)	180 milliliters
1 cup (16 tablespoons)	250 milliliters
1 pint (2 cups)	500 milliliters
1 quart (4 cups)	1 liter (about)

WEIGHT CONVERSIONS

US Weight Measure	Metric Equivalent
1/2 ounce	15 grams
1 ounce	30 grams
2 ounces	60 grams
3 ounces	85 grams
1/4 pound (4 ounces)	115 grams
1/2 pound (8 ounces)	225 grams
3/4 pound (12 ounces)	340 grams
1 pound (16 ounces)	454 grams

OVEN TEMPERATURE CONVERSIONS

Degrees Fahrenheit	Degrees Celsius
200 degrees F	95 degrees C
250 degrees F	120 degrees C
275 degrees F	135 degrees C
300 degrees F	150 degrees C
325 degrees F	160 degrees C
350 degrees F	180 degrees C
375 degrees F	190 degrees C
400 degrees F	205 degrees C
425 degrees F	220 degrees C
450 degrees F	230 degrees C

BAKING PAN SIZES

American	Metric
8 × 1½ inch round baking pan	20 × 4 cm cake tin
9 × 1½ inch round baking pan	23 × 3.5 cm cake tin
11 × 7 × 1½ inch baking pan	28 × 18 × 4 cm baking tin
13 × 9 × 2 inch baking pan	30 × 20 × 5 cm baking tin
2 quart rectangular baking dish	30 × 20 × 3 cm baking tin
15 × 10 × 2 inch baking pan	30 × 25 × 2 cm baking tin (Swiss roll tin)
9 inch pie plate	22 × 4 or 23 × 4 cm pie plate
7 or 8 inch springform pan	18 or 20 cm springform or loose bottom cake tin
9 × 5 × 3 inch loaf pan	23 × 13 × 7 cm or 2 lb narrow loaf or pate tin
1½ quart casserole	1.5 liter casserole
2 quart casserole	2 liter casserole

INDEX